25

BRIDGE CONVENTIONS

YOU

SHOULD KNOW

BARBARA SEAGRAM & MARC SMITH

25
BRIDGE CONVENTIONS
YOU
SHOULD KNOW

BARBARA SEAGRAM & MARC SMITH

MASTER POINT PRESS
TORONTO

Master Point Press
22 Lower Village Gate
Toronto, Ontario Canada
M5P 3L7
(416) 932-9766
Internet www.pathcom.com/~raylee/

Distributed in the USA by Barricade Books
150 Fifth Avenue, Suite 700
New York, NY 10011
(800) 59-BOOKS

Canadian Cataloguing in Publication Data
Smith, Marc, 1960-
25 bridge conventions you should know

ISBN 1-894154-07-X

1. Contract bridge — Bidding. I. Seagram, Barbara. II. Title. III. Title: 25 bridge conventions you should know.

GV1282.4.S64 1999   795.41'52   C98-932699-3

Editor	Ray Lee
Cover and Interior design	Olena S. Sullivan

Printed and bound in Canada

5 6 7   06 05 04 03 02 01

To my wonderful husband, Alex Kornel — my partner in life, in business, and at the table — with all my love.

Barbara

To the most important people in my life: my wife Charlotte, my dog Georgio, and all the bridge partners who have patiently suffered my idiosyncracies over the years.

Marc

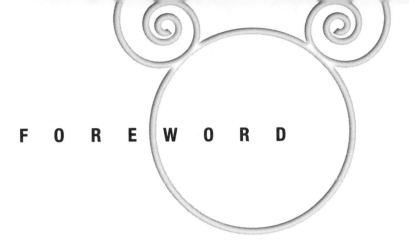

F O R E W O R D

I have just read a good bridge book, a very good bridge book — the one you have in your hands. I don't know whether everyone who writes a foreword reads the book as thoroughly as I have this one, but I did, and you have a treat in store for yourself.

You are about to familiarize yourself with twenty-five of the most popular and useful bidding conventions described succinctly, simply, and clearly — very clearly. Barbara Seagram and Marc Smith, a Canadian and a Brit, an unlikely pairing, have come up with a winner.

My gut feeling is that a reader who knows nothing or next to nothing about the convention being explained will leave the chapter thinking he or she can play the convention. It doesn't get any better than that.

In addition to the clarity of the explanations, and to my mind the most important feature of the book, a review-type quiz follows each chapter which further hammers home the important concepts. The summary of the main points contained in the chapter, which is laid out neatly before each quiz, is the icing on the cake.

I'm a bridge teacher and I'm going to recommend this book to my students. What more can I say other than that by hook or by crook you should make sure your partner also has a copy of this book? It still takes two to tango.

Eddie Kantar

ACKNOWLEDGEMENTS

My sincere thanks to an incredible teacher, Michael Davey, who taught me to love this game; to my dear friend and mentor, Eddie Kantar, whose books, friendship and humor have inspired my teaching for twenty years; to Alan LeBendig, the kindest and best friend ever, who is always there to give advice, wisdom and support; and to a great lady, Kate Buckman, who started the Kate Buckman Bridge Studio in Toronto in 1958 and who invited me to work for her in 1975; Kate taught me the magic of running a bridge club. My sincere thanks to all the thousands of students and members of our Studio who have taught me to learn and who have been so supportive over all the years. And last but not least, my thanks to our editor, Ray Lee, who made this book possible.

Barbara Seagram

I'd like to thank Eddie Kantar for his kind words in the Foreword, and for his many helpful suggestions on the manuscript. Eddie's comments were particularly useful in regard to the example hands, a number of which were improved considerably as a result of his input.

Marc Smith

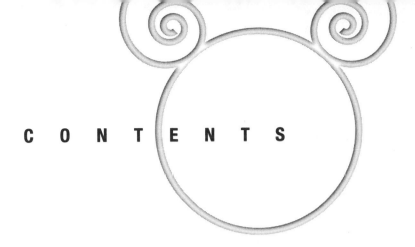

C O N T E N T S

A U T H O R S '   N O T E

In the course of this book, we frequently refer to 'points'. If you are bidding notrump, then this means high-card points (HCP) since you cannot count distribution for notrump purposes. However, when bidding suits, 'points' means total points (HCP + distributional points) unless we specifically say 'HCP'.

The opposition are referred to as LHO (left-hand opponent) and RHO (right-hand opponent). When partner opens the bidding, RHO bids next, then you, followed by LHO, and then partner again. If in doubt, refer to this diagram:

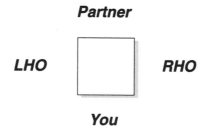

Throughout this book, you will see the terms 'natural' and 'artificial'. Describing a bid as natural means that, for instance, if you bid spades, it shows spades. An artificial (or conventional) bid, on the other hand, is quite different. For example, you might make a conventional club bid, and doing so may say nothing about your club holding. Your bid could show both majors, or ask your partner a question about his hand, or mean something else entirely, but it does not necessarily show the suit you have actually bid — hence the term 'artificial'.

Finally, we apologize to the politically correct amongst you for using the male pronoun exclusively throughout the book, for convenience. At all times you can assume that 'he' means 'he or she'.

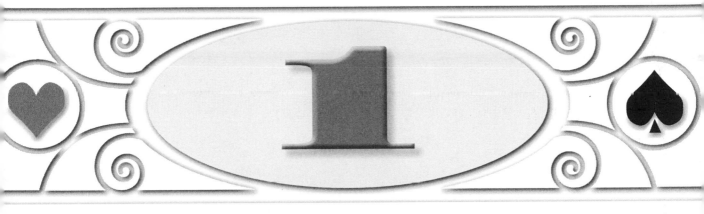

LEARN THESE
FIRST

C H A P T E R 1

STAYMAN 2♣ response to a 1NT opening

WHAT'S IN A NAME?

♥**Samuel M. Stayman** (1909-1993) was Life Master #48. He first described the convention that bears his name in 1945 in an article in *The Bridge World*, but it was actually invented by his partner, **George Rapee**! Stayman was world champion three times, and won twenty North American championship titles. The Stayman convention is one of only two (Blackwood being the other) that are used in some form by just about every partnership from beginners to world champions.

The Stayman convention allows you to find 4-4 major suit fits after you or your partner has opened 1NT and helps you to choose the right contract with a five-card major and invitational values. Major suits usually play better than notrump when you have at least an 8-card fit.

Stayman is a 2♣ response to an opening 1NT bid that has nothing to do with clubs, but instead asks opener — 'Do you have a four-card major?'

Partner	*You*
1NT	2♣

Note that there are two main
ways of playing Stayman, and
both work equally well provided
that both you and partner know
which one you are using. If you
prefer to play that a 2♥ response
shows four hearts and denies four
spades, and that 2♠ shows four
spades and may also have four
hearts, there's nothing wrong with
that. In this book, we assume
you are playing the set of
responses we recommend
in the text.

Opener's responses are easy to remember:

2♦	'I have no four-card major'
2♥	'I have four hearts and I may also have four spades'
2♠	'I have four spades but I do not have four hearts'

NO OTHER RESPONSES ARE ALLOWED

When can I use Stayman?

Once you have bid Stayman, you have committed your partnership to getting at least as high as 2NT. Since partner's 2♦ response doesn't promise diamonds, you can't just pass it out of fright! The basic requirements are:

- 8+ high-card points (i.e. at least invitational values)
- at least one four-card major
- a short suit (i.e. you should not use Stayman with 4-3-3-3 shape)

Stayman on game-forcing hands

If you have a hand with enough values to bid game, and one or two 4-card majors, Stayman is an invaluable tool to help you decide on the right contract over partner's 1NT opening. If he responds showing a fit in a four-card major that you own, then you raise to game in that suit. If he responds 2♦ denying a major, you bid 3NT. Whatever happens, you will reach the best game.

With two four-card majors, opener should convert to your known suit if necessary. Suppose his hand is:

♠ A J 6 2   ♥ K Q 5 2   ♦ K Q 5   ♣ 7 3

Partner	You
1NT	2♣
2♥	3NT
4♠	pass

This auction illustrates that it is on
the second round of bidding that
you tell partner which level is
appropriate for your combined
values. Here, you want to play in
game but have no slam interest,
so you jump right to game. You
should have a hand worth about
11-15 points.

As usual, 2♣ asked if partner had a four-card major and 2♥ showed that suit. This time you showed enough values for game by jumping to 3NT. Holding four spades as well as four hearts, partner converted 3NT to 4♠.

Stayman on invitational hands

You should use Stayman any time you have a four-card major and invitational values, unless you are 4-3-3-3. There are three possible outcomes:

1. Partner denies a four-card major

Partner	You
1NT	2♣
2♦	2NT
pass	

You ask if partner has a four-card major and 2♦ says 'No'. You now show an invitational hand by rebidding 2NT. With a minimum partner passes (with a maximum he will bid 3NT). This sequence has the same meaning as when you bid 2NT directly over the opening 1NT ('bid game with a maximum, partner').

2. Partner bids the major you were looking for

Partner	You
1NT	2♣
2♠	3♠
4♠	pass

You ask if partner has a four-card major and his 2♠ shows a four-card suit. You now show an invitational hand with four-card support by raising to 3♠. This time partner is maximum for his 1NT opening so he accepts the invitation.

3. Partner bids the 'wrong' major

If you were looking for a heart fit, and partner's response to Stayman is 2♠, then you will simply invite game in notrump. You know he doesn't have four hearts. But what if partner responds 2♥ when you were looking for a spade fit? He can still have four spades. The answer is that it's up to partner to tell you now. You simply raise notrump

BY THE WAY

Throughout this book we shall use terms such as 'weak', 'invitational' and 'game-forcing' to describe the strength of a hand. When partner has opened a 15-17 point 1NT, these are the categories for you as responder: 0-7 points is 'weak', which means that you have no game interest; 8-9 points is 'invitational': you have game interest if partner is maximum; a 'game-forcing' hand has 10+ points.

BY THE WAY

Remember that responding 2♠ to Stayman shows four spades and at the same time denies four hearts.

as before. Once again, the continuations are the same whether partner responds 2♦ or 2♥. Remember that you promised at least one four-card major when you bid 2♣ over the opening 1NT. You don't have hearts, so if partner has both majors he knows there is a 4-4 spade fit. He will place the contract in spades at the appropriate level.

Partner	You
1NT	2♣
2♥	2NT
3♠	pass

Stayman in the slam zone

Partner	You
1NT	2♣
2♠	4NT
?	

BY THE WAY

This does not mean that you cannot find out how many aces partner has once you have used Stayman. Later in this book (Chapter 6) we shall describe the Gerber convention, a bid of 4♣ over a 1NT opening used to ask for aces. This convention still applies after using Stayman — i.e. a sequence such as 1NT-2♣-2♥-4♣ is still Gerber.

You are probably familiar with the auction 1NT-4NT, which invites opener to pass with a minimum or to bid 6NT with a maximum. This is called a *quantitative raise* and shows about 16 points.

This sequence is exactly the same except that we have sidetracked to check on majors. 4NT in this auction is not Blackwood, therefore. It is exactly the same quantitative raise it would have been if Stayman had not entered the auction. You have bid 2♣ first in order to discover whether there is a 4-4 heart fit. There isn't, so you invite to slam in notrump.

Other invitational Stayman sequences

Remember that over 1NT, a direct bid of 2♥ or 2♠ shows five or more of the major but is a 'drop dead' bid. Stayman is useful for handling hands with a five-card major suit and invitational values.

Partner	You
1NT	2♣
2♦	2♥

This sequence shows invitational values and 5+ hearts. Partner can pass 2♥, convert to 2NT, or bid game in hearts or notrump, all of which you will pass.

Stayman on weak hands

A few pages back, we said that responder must have at least invitational values (8+ points) to bid 2♣ over 1NT. There are two exceptions to this:

♠ J 8 5 3   ♥ Q 9 7 6   ♦ Q 10 8 6 3   ♣ —

This hand certainly does not have invitational values but it does have a safety net. If opener responds 2♥ or 2♠, then you are happy to pass. If he doesn't have a four-card major then he will bid 2♦ and you can safely pass that too since he must have at least two diamonds to open 1NT.

Unfortunately, by assigning a conventional meaning to a 2♣ response to 1NT, you've lost the natural use of the bid, which is to show a weak hand with clubs. So now what do you do with

♠ 7 6   ♥ 8   ♦ J 10 3 2   ♣ Q 9 8 6 4 2

You bid Stayman anyway! And you rebid 3♣ over opener's response. Partner must pass. Notice that with this hand type, you do not need to have a major to bid Stayman, since you are planning on rebidding 3♣ to sign off. However, if you have a four-card major as well as your clubs, bidding Stayman gives you a chance of finding a major-suit fit and getting out at the two-level.

> **BY THE WAY**
>
> *You may also choose to bid Stayman and pass any response holding a 4-4-4-1 shape or with 4-3-5-1 or 3-4-5-1 (all with club singletons), but this will sometimes backfire. For example, if you bid 2♣ with 4-4-4-1 and pass 2♦, opener may have a 3-3-2-5 shape and 2♦ will be a silly contract.*

One more thing...

There is one final sequence that should be mentioned.

You	Partner
1NT	2♣
2♦	3♥

What do you think partner has this time?

Since he jumped to the three-level, he must have values for game, so you cannot pass. Why didn't he bid 3♥ directly over 1NT, though? The answer is that not only does he have at least five hearts, but he also has four spades. Something like:

♠ K Q 7 4   ♥ K J 8 6 2   ♦ K 6   ♣ 10 8

Partner bid Stayman to find out whether you had four spades. Once that possibility was gone (after your 2♦ response), he jumped to 3♥, asking you to choose between 4♥ and 3NT. He could also use the same sequence on a much stronger hand with slam interest, in which case he'll bid again once he knows whether you have three hearts.

✓ Responder must have at least one four-card major.

✓ Responder should not use Stayman with 4-3-3-3 shape.

✓ Responder must have at least 8HCP to use Stayman unless he can handle every response. This means that with 4-4-5-0 (or in very rare cases 4-4-4-1, 3-4-5-1, or 4-3-5-1), or long clubs (see below) it is okay to use Stayman with fewer than 8 HCP.

✓ Opener must respond to Stayman. He responds 2♦ (no four-card major), 2♥ (four hearts and maybe four spades too) or 2♠ (four spades and definitely not four hearts). Passing 2♣ is not an option.

✓ With both majors, opener responds 2♥, and should convert to spades if responder does not raise hearts (unless responder rebids 3♣ — see next point).

✓ With a weak hand, including six or more clubs, responder can use Stayman, then rebid 3♣. Opener must pass this.

✓ Responder must bid the full value of his hand on the second round by bidding or inviting game or slam. Without interest in game, responder may also pass opener's response to Stayman.

✓ A 4NT bid immediately after a response to Stayman is a quantitative raise. It does not ask for aces.

✓ After 1NT-2♣-2♦, a 2♥ or 2♠ rebid by the Stayman bidder is invitational with at least a five-card suit.

STAYMAN 2♣ RESPONSE TO 1NT

NOW TRY THESE...

1. On each of these hands, partner opens 1NT (15-17 points). What do you respond? If you decide to bid Stayman 2♣, what do you intend to do over each of partner's three possible responses?

<table>
<tr>
<td>a</td>
<td>♠ K J 7 3
♥ J 5 3 2
♦ A 3
♣ 10 8 6</td>
<td>b</td>
<td>♠ K J 3 2
♥ J 7
♦ 8 6 3
♣ K J 5 3</td>
<td>c</td>
<td>♠ K J 7 3 2
♥ 8
♦ K 7 4 2
♣ A Q 2</td>
</tr>
<tr>
<td>d</td>
<td>♠ K J 7 3 2
♥ A J 5 2
♦ Q 3
♣ 10 6</td>
<td>e</td>
<td>♠ K J 7 3 2
♥ 8
♦ 8 7 4 2
♣ J 6 2</td>
<td>f</td>
<td>♠ K J 7 3
♥ J 5 3 2
♦ 7 3
♣ 10 8 6</td>
</tr>
<tr>
<td>g</td>
<td>♠ J 7 6 3
♥ Q 8 7 3
♦ J 9 8 5 2
♣ —</td>
<td>h</td>
<td>♠ K J 7 3 2
♥ 8 2
♦ K 7 4
♣ J 6 2</td>
<td>i</td>
<td>♠ A 7 3 2
♥ K 8 2
♦ A J 4
♣ 7 6 2</td>
</tr>
</table>

2. This time you are opener. What do you bid next in each case?

<table>
<tr>
<td>a</td>
<td colspan="2">♠KQ4 ♥A642 ♦KQ5 ♣J74</td>
<td>b</td>
<td colspan="2">♠KQ7 ♥A642 ♦KQ53 ♣J4</td>
</tr>
<tr>
<td></td>
<td>You</td>
<td>Partner</td>
<td></td>
<td>You</td>
<td>Partner</td>
</tr>
<tr>
<td></td>
<td>1NT</td>
<td>2♣</td>
<td></td>
<td>1NT</td>
<td>2♣</td>
</tr>
<tr>
<td></td>
<td>2♥</td>
<td>3♥</td>
<td></td>
<td>2♥</td>
<td>2NT</td>
</tr>
<tr>
<td></td>
<td>?</td>
<td></td>
<td></td>
<td>?</td>
<td></td>
</tr>
</table>

<table>
<tr>
<td>c</td>
<td colspan="2">♠KQ74 ♥A642 ♦KQ5 ♣J4</td>
<td>d</td>
<td colspan="2">♠KQ74 ♥A642 ♦KQJ ♣J4</td>
</tr>
<tr>
<td></td>
<td>You</td>
<td>Partner</td>
<td></td>
<td>You</td>
<td>Partner</td>
</tr>
<tr>
<td></td>
<td>1NT</td>
<td>2♣</td>
<td></td>
<td>1NT</td>
<td>2♣</td>
</tr>
<tr>
<td></td>
<td>2♥</td>
<td>3♣</td>
<td></td>
<td>2♥</td>
<td>2♠</td>
</tr>
<tr>
<td></td>
<td>?</td>
<td></td>
<td></td>
<td>?</td>
<td></td>
</tr>
</table>

<table>
<tr>
<td>e</td>
<td colspan="2">♠KQ94 ♥A104 ♦KQJ2 ♣J4</td>
<td>f</td>
<td colspan="2">♠KQJ4 ♥A104 ♦KQJ2 ♣J4</td>
</tr>
<tr>
<td></td>
<td>You</td>
<td>Partner</td>
<td></td>
<td>You</td>
<td>Partner</td>
</tr>
<tr>
<td></td>
<td>1NT</td>
<td>2♣</td>
<td></td>
<td>1NT</td>
<td>2♣</td>
</tr>
<tr>
<td></td>
<td>2♠</td>
<td>3♥</td>
<td></td>
<td>2♠</td>
<td>4NT</td>
</tr>
<tr>
<td></td>
<td>?</td>
<td></td>
<td></td>
<td>?</td>
<td></td>
</tr>
</table>

<table>
<tr>
<td>g</td>
<td colspan="2">♠KQJ ♥A104 ♦KQJ42 ♣J4</td>
<td>h</td>
<td colspan="2">♠KQJ ♥A104 ♦KQJ42 ♣J4</td>
</tr>
<tr>
<td></td>
<td>You</td>
<td>Partner</td>
<td></td>
<td>You</td>
<td>Partner</td>
</tr>
<tr>
<td></td>
<td>1NT</td>
<td>2♣</td>
<td></td>
<td>1NT</td>
<td>2♣</td>
</tr>
<tr>
<td></td>
<td>2♦</td>
<td>3♣</td>
<td></td>
<td>2♦</td>
<td>2♠</td>
</tr>
<tr>
<td></td>
<td>?</td>
<td></td>
<td></td>
<td>?</td>
<td></td>
</tr>
</table>

ANSWERS

1 **a** 2♣ You will bid 2NT over a 2♦ response and raise a response of either major to the 3-level to show an invitational hand.

b 2♣ You will bid 2NT over a 2♦/2♥ response and raise a 2♠ response to the 3-level.

c 3♠ You have a game-forcing hand with a 5-card major and so do not need Stayman.

d 2♣ This time you use Stayman in case you have a 4-4 heart fit. You will raise a response of either major to game, and bid 3♠ over 2♦ (forcing and showing five spades and four hearts).

e 2♠ You have a five-card major and a weak hand, so do not use Stayman. Knowing partner has four hearts will not help you.

f pass While 2♥ or 2♠ might be a better contract than 1NT if partner has a four-card major, you cannot handle a 2♦ response to Stayman.

g 2♣ You intend to pass any response.

h 2♣ You will raise a 2♠ response to 3♠, and over either a 2♦ or 2♥ response you will bid an invitational 2♠ showing your five-card suit.

i 3NT Never use Stayman with 4-3-3-3 distribution.

2 **a** pass With a flat 15 points, you have no excuse for accepting partner's invitation.

b pass Partner is inviting, but you have a minimum.

c pass Partner wants to play 3♣, and he's not promising spades.

d 4♠ Partner has invitational values with five spades, and your hand has a fourth spade and 16 HCP.

e 4♥ This is just the same as the situation in (d). Partner has five hearts and is inviting game. You have 16 high, three good hearts and a ruffing value. Go for it!

f 6NT *4NT isn't Blackwood!* Partner has four hearts, and having failed to find a fit in that suit has invited you to slam in notrump. Your 17 points look great.

g pass We know, you have a great 17 and you don't like clubs much. So what?

h 4♠ Partner shows an invitational hand in this sequence. You have a maximum with three good spades. Just do it.

TAKEOUT DOUBLES

WHAT'S IN A NAME?

♥The idea of using a double for takeout instead of penalties originated around 1912, in the days of auction bridge. At that time it was called an 'informatory double'. One of the inventors was **Bryant McCampbell** *(d. about 1930)* of St. Louis, who was also responsible for creating the 4-3-2-1 point-count system we still use today.

Strictly speaking, when you make the call of 'double' it says that you believe the opponents have bid too much and have arrived at a contract you think will fail. It signifies confidence that you will collect a penalty and that you wish to double the stakes for which the hand is played. This traditional 'penalty' or 'business' double is still very handy when you think the opponents are overboard.

LHO	*Partner*	*RHO*	*You*
1♦	dbl		

However, in many common bidding situations such as this one, there are other (much more valuable) uses for the call 'double'. We shall be looking at a number of these alternatives throughout this book, but the first, and the most commonly encountered throughout the bridge-playing world, is the **takeout double**.

You have the following hand:

♠ A J 7 4   ♥ K Q 8 3   ♦ 5   ♣ K J 9 6

Your RHO (right hand opponent) opens the bidding with 1♦. You cannot make an overcall, because you do not have a five-card suit. You don't really want to pass and let the opponents have the hand cheaply when you have a nice opening bid yourself. So, what can you do? You would like to have a magic word that will force partner to bid his best suit. The answer to this conundrum is that you do have such a magic word, and that word is 'double'. You give up very little by assigning this meaning to a double in this kind of auction, since you will only very rarely have a hand on which you want to double 1♦ for penalties.

How do you know when a double is for takeout?

The $64,000 question. These are the four rules for making a basic takeout double:

1. *The bidding is at a level below game.*

2. *The doubler has not made a call other than pass.*

3. *The doubler's partner has not made a call other than pass.*

4. *The opponents have bid a suit (not notrump).*

If a double fits *all* of these requirements, it is a takeout double. For now, all other doubles are for penalties. The double in each of the following auctions is for takeout. Note how in each case the double meets all of the requirements above:

Auction 1

LHO	Partner	RHO	You
1♥	dbl		

Auction 2

LHO	Partner	RHO	You
1♥	pass	2♥	dbl

Auction 3

LHO	Partner	RHO	You
1♥	pass	pass	dbl

Auction 4

LHO	Partner	RHO	You
3♥	dbl		

By contrast, the final double in each of the *following* auctions is not for takeout:

Auction 5

LHO	Partner	RHO	You
	1NT	2♥	dbl

This is not for takeout as partner has bid.

Auction 6

LHO	Partner	RHO	You
1NT	dbl		

You cannot double a notrump opening for takeout. This is a penalty double, showing 16+ points.

Auction 7

LHO	Partner	RHO	You
4♠	dbl		

You cannot make a takeout double of a game bid, therefore this double is for penalties.

Auction 8

LHO	Partner	RHO	You
			1♥
pass	1♠	2♣	dbl

This double is not for takeout for two reasons: partner has made a bid other than pass, and so have you.

What do you need to
make a takeout double?

There are three types of hand on which you can make a takeout double. What can be regarded as a 'normal takeout double' is by far the most common of these three hand types and has the following requirements:

1. *A hand worth at least an opening bid.*

2. *Adequate trump support for all of the unbid suits (at least Jxx).*

3. *Shortness in the opponents' suit (at most a doubleton).*

A normal takeout double shows at least opening strength in terms of high-card points and asks partner to choose his best unbid suit. There is essentially no upper limit for your strength, as we shall see later.

Note that, once again, your hand must fit all the requirements to qualify as a double. If you have no good alternative (such as a decent five-card suit that you can overcall), and lack adequate trump support for all unbid suits, then you must pass even though you have an opening bid.

♠ A K 7 4   ♥ 8 4   ♦ A 9 2   ♣ Q 9 6 3

LHO	Partner	RHO	You
		1♦	?

On this hand, then, you may not say 'double'. Partner is likely to bid hearts, after which bidding a new suit would show a much better hand than this (as we'll see shortly). Partner will not approve if this hand comes down as dummy in a heart contract since you have promised support (at least Jxx) for all the unbid suits.

The other two hand types that you may have for a takeout double are two types of hand that are too strong to start with any other bid:

1. *A strong one-suited hand* (16+ points and a 6-card suit, or 19+ points and a 5-card suit)

2. *A hand too strong to overcall 1NT* (19+ points and a balanced hand)

We shall see later how you tell partner you have one of these hands rather than a normal takeout double.

How do you respond when partner
makes a takeout double?

Always remember this saying: *Takeout doubles are to be taken out.* If there is no intervening bid then you *must* respond to partner's takeout double, however bad your hand. You must bid your favorite unbid suit even if you have no points. In fact, *especially* if you have no points!

♠ J 8 6 3   ♥ 9 7 4 3   ♦ 4 3 2   ♣ 6 2

LHO	Partner	RHO	You
1♥	dbl	pass	?

You have very few high cards on this hand, but that does not mean you can pass partner's double. To understand why, think about what passing really means — you're opting to defend 1♥ doubled. That means you think your side can take more than half of the tricks with hearts as trumps. It is equivalent to playing the hand as declarer in a heart contract. Bearing in mind that you can expect partner to have a singleton heart, would you like to be declarer in a heart contract? Of course not, and so you should choose your best of the three unbid suits as partner has requested — in this case you bid 1♠.

Responding to the double is not quite as simple as choosing your best suit. You also need to tell partner if you have a good hand. Assuming your RHO passes partner's double, you should respond as follows:

0-8 points   bid your best suit at the cheapest level
9-11 points   bid your best suit one level higher than necessary or bid notrump (see below)
12+ points   force to game

These point ranges are high-card points plus distributional points (based on the guarantee that partner has support for your longest suit). Effectively, partner has already bid your longest suit and you are now supporting him.

If you have 9-11 points and partner makes a takeout double, you need to let him know that there is a chance of game. You make the same suit response that you would with a worse hand, but bid it one level higher.

♠ K J 8 3   ♥ 5 2   ♦ A 5 4 2   ♣ Q 8 4

LHO	Partner	RHO	You
1♥	dbl	pass	2♠

With fewer high cards (without the ♦A, for example), you would simply respond 1♠. With a hand in this range, however, jump to 2♠ to describe your values.

If you have 12+ points opposite partner's takeout double then you both have an opening bid, which means that you want to reach game. If you have a five-card major, bid game in that suit. If you do not, then make the lowest available bid in the opponent's suit. This is an artificial bid called a **cuebid** which says nothing about that suit but simply tells partner to keep bidding until you can decide where to play the hand.

Following the cuebid, you both bid your best suits until either you find one you both like (and then someone can bid game in it) or you find that you have no suit that you both like (in which case you'll likely end up in 3NT).

To understand how this works, look at the following auction:

Partner	You
♠ K Q 9 6	♠ A J 8 3
♥ A Q 8 4	♥ K 7 3
♦ 5	♦ Q 8 5 2
♣ Q 9 7 6	♣ K 5

LHO	Partner	RHO	You
1♦	dbl	pass	2♦[1]
pass	2♥[2]	pass	3♠[3]
pass	4♠[4]	all pass	

1. I have some values but no five-card major

2. I have four hearts

3. I have four spades and a good hand

4. So do I

When should you bid notrump in response to partner's double?

With 8+ points you should prefer to respond in notrump if you do not have a four-card major to show. Of course, you must also have a stopper in the opponent's suit to bid notrump!

Notrump responses to a takeout double

8-10 points, 1 stopper in opponents' suit	*bid cheapest level of NT*
11-12 points, 1½ stoppers in opponents' suit	*jump in NT*
13+ points, 1½ stoppers in opponents' suit	*bid 3NT*

♠ 9 3　　♥ 9 7 6 5 4　　♦ 7 5 3　　♣ J 8 3

LHO	Partner	RHO	You
1♥	dbl	pass	?

As we mentioned earlier, you cannot bid 1NT in response to a takeout double just because you don't like any of the three unbid suits. The 1NT response shows 8-10 HCP and a stopper.

Many players make the mistake of bidding 1NT on this type of hand, but you must not. Partner asked you to pick your best suit, not your best four-card suit, so bid 2♣. When your only long suit is the opponents' suit, make your cheapest bid in a three-card suit.

By contrast, on this hand you *should* bid 1NT in the above auction:

♠ K 9 3　　♥ Q 9 7 6　　♦ J 7 5　　♣ A 8 5

What if opener's partner bids?

LHO	Partner	RHO	You
1♥	dbl	2♥	?

If there is an intervening bid following partner's takeout double, whether it's a new suit or not, you are off the hook. You are now perfectly free to pass whenever you have a poor hand.   In fact, since you are not forced to respond, when you do so you are promising some values — this is called making a 'free bid', and promises at least 8 points or so.

What about rebids by the takeout doubler?

With 13-15 points, a minimum hand for your double, you should not bid again if partner has simply responded by bidding his best suit at the cheapest level. However, with extra values you can raise partner's suit. For example, here:

♠ K J 8 6　　♥ K J 4　　♦ 5 3　　♣ A J 7 3

LHO	Partner	RHO	You
		1♦	dbl
pass	1♠	pass	?

You should pass. You have 14 points and partner has 0-8. Game is impossible.

♠ A Q 8 6   ♥ K Q 4   ♦ 5 3   ♣ A Q 7 6

LHO	Partner	RHO	You
		1♦	dbl
pass	1♠	pass	?

This time bid 2♠. You have 18 points and partner has 0-8. Game is possible if partner has close to a maximum.

♠ A Q J 6   ♥ A K 4   ♦ 5 3   ♣ A J 6 3

LHO	Partner	RHO	You
		1♦	dbl
pass	1♠	pass	?

This hand is worth a jump to 3♠. You have twenty points and partner has 0-8. Partner should raise to game with any excuse at all.

♠ A K J 6   ♥ A K 4   ♦ 5   ♣ A K J 6 3

LHO	Partner	RHO	You
		1♦	dbl
pass	1♠	pass	?

Just bid 4♠ on this monster. You have 22+ points and game is possible even when partner has almost nothing. If partner has any five spades or as little as the ♥Q or the ♣Q, game is very likely to make.

The other time you may bid again over partner's response is when you have one of the two strong hand types mentioned earlier, rather than a normal take-out double.

♠ K 5   ♥ A Q J 8 6 3   ♦ A 5   ♣ K Q 5

LHO	Partner	RHO	You
		1♦	dbl
pass	1♠	pass	?

Bid 2♥. Your hand is too strong simply to overcall 1♥ on the first round, so you make a takeout double first. Partner will respond on the assumption that you have a normal takeout double, but you tell him you have a strong one-suited hand by bidding your own suit on the second round of bidding. While partner isn't forced to bid on over this, he will make every effort to do so, knowing you have a very big hand.

♠ K Q 5 ♥ A J 8 4 ♦ A Q 10 ♣ K J 9

LHO	Partner	RHO	You
		1♦	dbl
pass	1♠	pass	?

Rebid 1NT. An immediate overcall of 1NT over 1♦ would have shown 15-18 points. By doubling first and then bidding notrump at the lowest available level you show a balanced hand with stoppers in the opponents' suit in the 18-20 point range. If you had the same hand with 21-22 points you would jump to 2NT after starting with a takeout double, and with 23+ you can bid 3NT on the second round.

So can you ever pass partner's takeout double?

Certainly you can — but very rarely. You are converting the takeout double into a penalty double — making a penalty pass, in fact.

♠ K 7 ♥ 9 3 ♦ Q J 10 8 7 5 ♣ Q 5 3

LHO	Partner	RHO	You
1♦	dbl	pass	

This is exactly the type of hand you need to pass partner's takeout double, and even with this you should still not be overly surprised if 1♦ doubled makes!

BY THE WAY

After this kind of auction (a penalty pass of a takeout double), a trump lead is mandatory if partner has one. You should have more trumps than they do, so start drawing them.

Summary

✓ A double is for takeout if *all* these conditions apply:

  — an opponent has opened the bidding with a suit bid

  — neither you nor partner has yet made a bid other than pass

  — the last bid is below game

✓ To make a takeout double you must have support for all unbid suits, shortness in the opponents' suit, and at least opening-bid values.

✓ You must respond to partner's takeout double, however weak your hand. If you do not have four cards in any of the unbid suits, bid your cheapest three-card suit.

✓ A notrump response shows positive values, not weakness.

✓ A jump response in a suit shows invitational values.

✓ A cuebid response is artificial and forcing.

✓ A pass can be used, very rarely, for penalties, with a very long and strong holding in the opponents' suit.

✓ With a minimum takeout double, the doubler must pass a minimum response; with extra values, he may bid again (for example, raise responder's suit).

✓ Doubling and then bidding a new suit shows a hand too strong for a simple overcall; doubling and then bidding notrump shows a hand too strong to overcall 1NT.

TAKEOUT DOUBLES

NOW TRY THESE...

What is your next bid on each of these hands?

1   ♠ AJ74 ♥ KQ96 ♦ 3 ♣ K874

LHO	Partner	RHO	You
		1♦	?

2   ♠ K4 ♥ KQ964 ♦ K4 ♣ Q1085

LHO	Partner	RHO	You
		1♦	?

3   ♠ AQJ875 ♥ AQ ♦ A4 ♣ J85

LHO	Partner	RHO	You
		1♥	?

4   ♠ A6 ♥ KQ86 ♦ AJ97 ♣ AK3

LHO	Partner	RHO	You
		1♦	?

5   ♠ KQ64 ♥ 62 ♦ K97 ♣ AJ73

LHO	Partner	RHO	You
		1♦	?

6   ♠ 97 ♥ 103 ♦ J9864 ♣ 9754

LHO	Partner	RHO	You
1♦	dbl	pass	?

7   ♠ Q10753 ♥ K4 ♦ 853 ♣ KJ6

LHO	Partner	RHO	You
1♦	dbl	pass	?

8   ♠ Q107 ♥ J5 ♦ KJ74 ♣ K964

LHO	Partner	RHO	You
1♦	dbl	pass	?

9   ♠ 5 ♥ KQ1085 ♦ A63 ♣ KJ74

LHO	Partner	RHO	You
1♦	dbl	pass	?

10   ♠ 65 ♥ KQ108 ♦ A63 ♣ KJ74

LHO	Partner	RHO	You
1♦	dbl	pass	?

11   ♠ AK85 ♥ K1098 ♦ 8 ♣ J974

LHO	Partner	RHO	You
		1♦	dbl
pass	1♠	pass	?

12   ♠ AQ5 ♥ KQ105 ♦ 63 ♣ KQ74

LHO	Partner	RHO	You
		1♦	dbl
pass	1♥	pass	?

ANSWERS

1   dbl   You have 15 points and support for all unbid suits.

2   1♥   You have a good five-card heart suit so should overcall rather than doubling.

3   dbl   You are too strong simply to overcall 1♠, so double and then bid spades on the next round.

4   dbl   You are too strong to overcall 1NT, so double and then bid notrump on the next round.

5   pass   You must have support for all the unbid suits to make a takeout double. You are not strong enough to bid 1NT, and you have no suit long and strong enough to overcall.

6   2♣   Pick your favorite of the three unbid suits. You must not pass partner's takeout double with this type of hand — you don't really think those diamonds are good enough to defend with, do you?

7   2♠   You have 10 points so you jump in your best suit.

8   1NT   You have 10 HCP, no four-card major, and a stopper in the opponents' suit. Perfect!

9   4♥   You have enough points for game, and partner has promised you heart support.

10   2♦   You have an opening bid, but it's not yet clear what the right game is. Let partner know right away by making a cuebid. If partner bids hearts you will raise, otherwise you can try notrump.

11   pass   Partner has a minimum, and so have you, despite your four-card spade support.

12   2♥   Just enough for a single raise. If partner is at the top of his range, game just might be there.

C H A P T E R **3**

WEAK TWO-BIDS

In the early days of bridge, an opening bid at the two-level was usually natural, and showed a very strong hand. The modern style is to use 2♣ as an all-purpose strong opening, and to reserve 2♦, 2♥ and 2♠ for hands that are a little weaker than an opening bid. We shall discuss auctions that begin with 2♣ in the next chapter.

What does a Weak Two-Bid look like?

6-10 high-card points and exactly a six-card suit. The six-card suit must include two of the top three honors or three of the top five honors.

The distribution of your hand should be 6-3-2-2, 6-3-3-1 or 6-4-2-1. You may not have a side four-card major. If your points including distribution add up to 13 or more, then your hand is too strong to open with a Weak Two-Bid — just open with one of your long suit.

BY THE WAY

In third seat only, you may relax the rules a bit for opening a Weak Two — your suit does not have to be quite so perfect.

These hands could all be opened with a Weak Two-Bid:

♠ A Q 8 6 4 3   ♥ J 6 3   ♦ 5 4   ♣ 3 2

♠ 5 2   ♥ K J 10 7 5 4   ♦ Q 7 4 2   ♣ 5

♠ K 5 3   ♥ 4   ♦ K Q 7 4 3 2   ♣ 6 3 2

These hands are not Weak Two-Bids:

♠ A Q 8 6 4 3   ♥ J 6 3 2   ♦ 5   ♣ 3 2   (side four-card major)

♠ A 2   ♥ K J 10 7 5 4   ♦ Q 7 4 2   ♣ 5   (too strong — open 1♥)

♠ K 5 3   ♥ 4   ♦ K 8 7 4 3 2   ♣ 6 3 2   (suit not good enough)

Weak Two-Bids can be compared to preemptive opening bids of 3♦, 3♥ and 3♠, except that the three-level bids show a seven-card suit while a Weak Two-Bid shows only a six-card suit.

Why use Weak Two-Bids?

In the first place, you're not giving up very much. The old fashioned rock-crusher two-bids don't occur that frequently, and as you'll see in the next chapter, they can be handled quite well by opening 2♣ anyway. The main reason for making a preemptive bid is to deprive the opponents of bidding space, thereby making their lives tough. However, since Weak Two-Bids describe your hand within fairly narrow parameters, they can also help partner decide whether to play or defend. The main advantages of Weak Two-bids are:

1. *They make life more difficult for the opponents who now have to come into the auction at a higher level.*

LHO	*RHO*
♠ 7 6	♠ A 9
♥ A Q 7	♥ K 6
♦ Q 9 8 6 3	♦ K 7 5 4 2
♣ K 7 6	♣ Q J 4 3

If RHO is the dealer and your side passes throughout, it is not hard to construct an auction that will get them to 5♦, a contract that is a heavy favorite to make. Now, let's change things slightly and say that you deal and open with a 2♠ bid. Life is now much harder and it is quite conceivable that neither opponent will bid at all. Worse still, you will probably even make 2♠!

2. *They direct the opening lead, in case you defend the hand.*

♠ K Q 10 9 8 2   ♥ 6 5   ♦ A 7 2   ♣ 7 3

If you pass, the player on your left opens 1NT and his partner raises to 3NT.

What lead do you think gives you the best chance of beating the opponent's game? Right — a spade. Partner has:

♠ J 4   ♥ K 10 8 6 3   ♦ 8 4   ♣ Q 6 4 2

Do you think he'll find a spade lead? Of course not. He will lead a heart and the opponents will score nine easy tricks. On a spade lead, they have virtually no chance. If you open 2♠, and the opponents still bid to 3NT, then partner will lead the ♣J and down will go the contract.

3.   *They are very descriptive bids which tell partner immediately your point range, the approximate shape of your hand, and the quality of your suit.*

When you are known to have a six-card suit of reasonable quality, it is a guaranteed source of tricks — this is often referred to as 'playing strength'. Since partner can now accurately envision your hand, the partnership may be able to reach a good game with fewer than 26 points.

Partner	*You*
♠ K J 10 8 6 3	♠ Q 7 2
♥ 3	♥ A 9 6 4
♦ K 6 4	♦ A 7
♣ 9 7 2	♣ A 9 6 4

Wouldn't you want to bid these two hands to 4♠? Your only losers will be two clubs and the ♠A, but with only 21 HCP between you it is not so easy a contract to reach. If you hold the East hand and are told that partner has seven points, you would not expect to be able to make game. However, if you are told that partner has seven points and a good six-card spade suit you might well take a different view of the hand.

What do you do when partner opens a Weak Two-Bid?

Always remember that partner has not got much — about 8 high-card points and a decent six-card suit. Even with good support for partner's suit, you need a good opening bid even to try for game. Of course, the better your support for partner, the less you need in terms of high-card points. By contrast, with no fit for partner, you should be very wary of bidding. When you have a singleton in partner's suit, you will often pass even with as much as 15 points. (Partner has a maximum of 10 points, so even if you have 15 you will probably not be able to make game with no fit for partner's suit).

Armed with these basic principles, let's look at your various options when partner opens a Weak Two-Bid.

How do you respond to a Weak Two-Bid?

1. Bid a new suit

Partner	You
2♠	3♥

This is a constructive action, and you should have a hand with some expectation of making game if you find a fit. But you should also expect partner to be short in your longest suit. To bid a new suit in response to partner's Weak Two-Bid you must have a minimum of 13+ points and a good five-card or longer suit of your own. The stronger and/or longer your own suit, the fewer high-card points you need. The bid of a new suit is forcing for one round — partner is not allowed to pass. Partner should raise your suit with three-card support, or failing that, bid his side suit. With no support for you and no side suit, partner rebids his long suit.

2. Raise opener's suit

Partner	You
2♠	3♠

Direct raises of partner's suit are to play: partner is not allowed to bid again. A raise of partner's suit to the three-level is made with a weak hand and three trumps, simply to increase the preempt. Here's a typical hand for this bid:

♠ J75　♥ 95　♦ A97643　♣ 953

Partner has 6-10 points and you have five. It is almost certain the opponents can make a game, and perhaps even a slam. Raise partner's opening 2♠ to 3♠ to make it harder for your LHO to come in.

Partner	You
2♠	4♠

This auction is especially difficult for the opponents, since you might have a very weak hand, like:

♠ 9753　♥ 5　♦ A97543　♣ 953

Since you have a ten-card trump fit, you should be prepared to compete to the four-level. Of course, you do not expect to make 4♠, but the opponents could easily be cold for a slam! On the other hand, you would make the same raise to 4♠ with something like

♠ Q974　♥ AKQ7　♦ 6　♣ KQ85

This time, of course, you expect to make 4♠. There is no chance that you will have missed a slam — partner cannot have as much as the ♠AK and another ace. Look how hard this makes things for your LHO. With the first hand above you bid 4♠ as a sacrifice, but this time you can expect to collect a juicy penalty if the opponents now come in at the five-level.

3. Ask for more information

Partner	You
2♠	2NT
3♦	

The bid of 2NT in response to a Weak Two-Bid opening is conventional. All it says about your hand is that you are at least interested in game. 2NT is forcing for one round and asks partner to bid any ace or king in a side suit. This is called 'asking for a feature'. Partner's 3♦ rebid in this example shows the ♦A or ♦K, but says nothing about length in the diamond suit. This is useful when you are the responder to a Weak Two-Bid and you have a hand with some 'holes'. It is nice to know whether partner's hand can fill in those holes. Remember, too, that if partner has values in your short suits, that is usually bad.

Let's say you have the following hand:

♠ Q 8 6   ♥ A Q 9 5   ♦ K Q 7 3   ♣ J 4

and partner opens with a weak 2♠. Wouldn't you like to know if partner has the ♥K or the ♦A? Either of these would be magic cards as they will provide you with a source of tricks. So, in response to partner's 2♠ opening you bid 2NT. If opener bids either 3♦ or 3♥, you can bid 4♠. If partner bids 3♣, you will bid 3♠ which opener must pass.

You may have a much better hand than this when you bid 2NT. You may know you are going to bid game anyway but want to see if partner has a particular card to make slam. For example:

♠ A 10 9 4   ♥ A K J 7 6 4   ♦ —   ♣ Q J 7

When partner opens a weak 2♠, you know that he has the ♠KQ (he has promised two of the top three honors or three of the top five). The only question is, does he have the ace or king of clubs? If he does, then you want to bid 6♠. If he does not, then it's very unlikely that you can make slam. Again, bidding 2NT will give you the information you need.

4. Pass

The action you will take on most hands without much of a fit for partner and where you are not interested in game. Stay out of the auction, and hope that the preempt has done its work.

WEAK TWO-BIDS

You cannot preempt in fourth seat. To understand why, think about why you preempt — to make life difficult for the opponents. Clearly, if the bidding starts with three passes and you have a bad hand, you should simply pass and move on to the next deal. Who knows, perhaps you will get a better hand next time around!

Summary

✓ To open a Weak Two-Bid you must have 6-10 points and a six-card suit headed by two of the top three honors or three of the top five.

✓ If your high-card points and your distributional points add up to 13, you are too strong for a Weak Two-Bid — open at the one-level.

✓ You may not open a Weak Two-Bid when you have a side four-card major, but you may do so holding a four-card minor.

✓ To make a (forcing) bid in a new suit in response to a Weak Two, you must have a good hand (at least 13 points and usually more) and a good five-card or longer suit .

✓ Any raise of a Weak Two-Bid is to play: opener may not bid again.

✓ With a weak hand and a fit, raise to continue the preempt. With three trumps, raise to the three-level, and with four trumps, raise to the four-level. A raise of opener's suit to game may be pre-emptive or may be bid to make.

✓ A 2NT response to a Weak Two-Bid asks opener to bid any ace or king in a side suit.

WEAK TWO-BIDS

1. You are dealer, with both side vulnerable. What do you bid on each of the following hands?

a ♠ 8 5
♥ A Q 10 7 5 3
♦ Q 7
♣ 9 6 3

b ♠ J 10 7 4
♥ K Q 10 8 5 3
♦ J 7
♣ 8

c ♠ K Q J 9 7 5 3
♥ 8 6
♦ J 7 4
♣ 7

d ♠ J 7 4
♥ 8 6 4
♦ K Q 9 8 4 3
♣ 7

e ♠ A J 8 7 4 3
♥ Q 6
♦ Q 8 5
♣ 8 5

f ♠ A J 10 7 4 3
♥ K 6
♦ Q J 5
♣ 8 5

2. With neither side vulnerable, partner opens a weak 2♠ and RHO passes What do you respond in each case?

a ♠ Q J
♥ K Q
♦ A K Q 8 5
♣ K J 8 5

b ♠ 4
♥ K Q 6 4
♦ K J 8 5 3
♣ A J 7

c ♠ Q J 2
♥ —
♦ A Q J 4 3
♣ A Q J 8 4

d ♠ 6 3
♥ A K Q 10 7
♦ A Q 5
♣ K 10 8

e ♠ K 7 4
♥ 8 6 4 3
♦ Q 9 6 3
♣ J 4

f ♠ J 8 7 4 3
♥ K 6
♦ Q 10 5
♣ 8 5 2

WEAK TWO-BIDS

ANSWERS

1   **a**   2♥   This is a perfect description of your hand.

     b   pass   You cannot open 2♥ with a four-card spade suit on the side.

     c   3♠   You cannot open a Weak Two-Bid on a seven-card suit.

     d   2♦   Your hand qualifies for a Weak Two-Bid in every respect.

     e   pass   You don't have two of the top three or three of the top five in spades.

     f   1♠   Count your points — you are too good to open with a pre-empt.

2   **a**   4♠   Partner must have the ♠AK and cannot therefore have either of the other missing aces, so there is no hope of slam.

     b   pass   With a singleton spade, despite your good hand, don't be surprised if 2♠ is too high.

     c   2NT   Partner must have the ♠AK. If he also has a minor-suit king then you will be able to count thirteen tricks and you can bid 7♠. If he does not, then you plan to settle for 6♠, which at worst will require one of the minor-suit finesses to work.

     d   3♥   You have too much not to bid game, but 4♥ may be the best contract. See whether partner can support your suit before making a decision.

     e   3♠   You expect the hand to belong to the opponents, but this little raise will make life that much tougher for them.

     f   4♠   If the red-suit honors are badly placed, you may have no tricks at all on defense! Raise the stakes as high as you dare right away, and let them start bidding at the five-level.

2♣ STRONG ARTIFICIAL OPENING

WHAT'S IN A NAME?

♥ Strong natural two-bids were part of both the Culbertson and Goren systems. Most modern systems have abandoned them in favor of other uses for 2♦, 2♥, and 2♠. However, the idea of using 2♣ as an all-purpose strong opening bid dates back to *David Burnstine (1900-1965)* of New York City, in 1929.

As we pointed out in the last chapter, if you are playing Weak Two-Bids rather than the old-style Strong Two's, then you must have a bid to show a very strong hand. That bid is an opening bid of 2♣, which is very strong, forcing and artificial — i.e. it says nothing about clubs. Essentially, two types of hand are opened 2♣ — balanced hands with 22+ HCP and unbalanced hands on which you want to insist on reaching game. Except in one situation that we shall discuss later, partner must keep the bidding open until game is reached, however bad his hand is.

What kind of hands do you open with 2♣?

1. *Any balanced hand with 22-25 HCP, or more than 28 HCP.*

2. *Very strong unbalanced hands.* To judge whether an unbalanced hand is worth a 2♣ bid, add your high-card points to your distributional points. If the total comes to those shown below, the hand is worth a 2♣ opening:

    21+ points and a seven-card suit

    23+ points and a six-card suit

    23+ points and two five-card suits

    25+ points and one five-card suit

With any of these hands, you open 2♣ and then bid your real suit next turn.

How do you respond when partner opens 2♣?

You will come across all kinds of different rules and methods of responding to a 2♣ opening. The scheme which we're going to describe here is both simple and commonly played, and we recommend that you adopt it until you come across something you like better.

Since the 2♣ opening demands that the bidding be kept alive until game is reached, there is plenty of time for you both to describe your hands accurately. However, because the opening bid has already used up the whole of the one-level, bids must be well defined.

Initial responses to 2♣

2♥/2♠/3♣/3♦   8 points and a good 5-card suit (at least two of the top three honors) or a 6-card suit (at least three of the top five honors)

2♦   Negative or waiting

If you have at least 8 HCP and a good five-card or longer suit, simply bid it. With anything else, you start off by bidding 2♦ and see what partner does next. In the old days, this bid was used to show a 'negative response' — a hand with less than four points or so. The modern style is to use 2♦ as a 'waiting bid' — you may still have either a good or a bad hand, you just don't have any suit good enough to bid directly. Let's say you have 10 high card points and a six-card heart suit headed by the jack. Clearly, with 10 points you do not have a negative response — this hand could easily be headed for the six- or seven-level. However, neither do you have a good suit headed by two of the top three honors. So you start with 2♦ simply to hear more from partner; you will introduce your suit at your next turn and then show your values in the subsequent auction. The 2♦ waiting bid denies a strong suit but not necessarily a strong hand.

What if you have a really bad hand as responder?

If you have three points or less (and no king in your hand), start by responding 2♦ as usual. But when partner bids his real suit, you now bid the cheaper minor (usually 3♣) to show a horrible hand — this is called a 'second negative'.

Partner		You	
2♣		2♦	(waiting)
2♠		3♣	(cheaper minor)

Partner		You	
2♣		2♦	(waiting)
3♣		3♦	(cheaper minor)

In these two example auctions, your second bid was **second negative**, letting partner know you have next to nothing. The only time you can't do this is when partner's real suit is diamonds:

Partner		You	
2♣		2♦	(waiting)
3♦		?	

Unfortunately, there is no way to show a really bad hand now. Partner should bear this in mind before deciding to open 2♣ on a hand where he's going to rebid diamonds.

How do you bid big balanced hands?

All balanced hands are handled by opening or rebidding notrump. With the addition of the opening 2♣ bid to your system, we can construct a complete table, as below. Remember that only high card points can be counted in evaluating balanced hands.

Notrump openings and rebids with balanced hands

HCP	Open	Rebid
12-14	1 of a suit	1NT
15-17	1NT	
18-19	1 of a suit	2NT
20-21	2NT	
22-23	2♣	2NT
24-25	2♣	3NT
26-27	3NT	
28+	2♣	4NT

When partner opens 2♣ and then rebids 2NT over your 2♦, you can use exactly the same methods as you do when he opens 2NT (remembering that partner's hand is now a little stronger). If you play Stayman 3♣ over a 2NT opening, then do so when the auction starts 2♣-2♦-2NT also. Similarly, Gerber and Transfers (Chapters 6 and 8), if you play them over 2NT, should be used here too.

We mentioned earlier that a 2♣ opening bid is forcing to game, but that there is (as usual) one exception to this rule. When opener starts with 2♣ and rebids 2NT over a 2♦ response, that shows 22-23 point balanced hand, and responder may pass with a completely worthless hand. (Consider the auction as though partner has opened with 2NT except he has now shown 22-23 HCP.)

How do you bid unbalanced hands after the first round or two?

Essentially, bidding is natural, but colored by the fact that you are forced to game. Let's look at one or two example auctions:

♠ 86   ♥ K J 7 3 2   ♦ A 8 2   ♣ 6 5 4

You	Partner
2♣	2♦
2♠	3♥

Partner has fewer than three spades, but at least five hearts. However, his hearts were not good enough for him to bid 2♥ directly over 2♣. You know he does have at least four points, though, or he would have bid 3♣ (second negative).

♠ J 6 3   ♥ A 8 7 3   ♦ K 8 5 2   ♣ Q 4

You	Partner
2♣	2♦
2♠	3♠

Partner has agreed spades, and is still unlimited — he could have a very good hand indeed. Since you are forced to game, neither of you has to worry about being passed out below 4♠. Now you have plenty of room to explore slam.

♠ 9 7 6 3   ♥ 7 3   ♦ Q J 2   ♣ 6 5 4 2

You	Partner
2♣	2♦
2♠	4♠

By contrast, this is a hand where you would have used a second negative if partner hadn't bid a suit you liked. The jump to game shows spade support, but no aces, kings, singletons, or voids — i.e. a lousy hand.

Summary

✓ A 2♣ opening is forcing to game (unless opener rebids 2NT). You can never pass below game, no matter how bad your hand may be.

✓ If balanced, opener must have at least 22 high card points to open 2♣.

✓ If unbalanced, opener needs 21+ points (high cards and distribution) with a 7-card suit, or more points with a less unbalanced hand.

✓ When partner opens 2♣, you may make a positive bid in a suit with 8+ HCP and a suit of five cards or more headed by at least two top honors (or a six-card suit headed by three of the top five honors).

✓ With neither of the above you should start with a 2♦ 'waiting' bid.

✓ With a worthless hand (three points or less and no king), make a 'second negative' by bidding your cheaper minor after opener rebids a suit (not available when he rebids 3♦).

✓ If opener rebids 2NT (showing 22-23 balanced), use whatever methods you would have used if he had opened 2NT.

2♣ STRONG ARTIFICIAL OPENING

NOW TRY THESE...

1. What is your opening bid on each of the following hands?

a ♠ K Q 9 5   *2C*
   ♥ A J 7
   ♦ A K
   ♣ K Q J 5

b ♠ A 5
   ♥ K Q J 10 7 6 2   *2C*
   ♦ A K J
   ♣ 5

c ♠ 3
   ♥ A 7
   ♦ A Q J 8 5   *1D*
   ♣ K Q J 10 6

d ♠ K J 3
   ♥ K Q 10   *2C*
   ♦ A K Q 5 3
   ♣ A K

e ♠ A K 8 6
   ♥ A K 4 2
   ♦ A K 7 4   *1D*
   ♣ 4

f ♠ A K 8 6 4 2
   ♥ 3   *1S*
   ♦ A K 8 5 3 2
   ♣ —

2. Partner opens 2♣. What is your response on each of the following hands?

a ♠ K Q 10 4 3   *2S*
   ♥ K J 5
   ♦ 9 5 2
   ♣ 7 2

b ♠ 8 5 2
   ♥ 9 6 3 2   *2D*
   ♦ 7
   ♣ J 7 4 3 2

c ♠ Q 9 8 6 4 3   *2D*
   ♥ A K 5
   ♦ 3
   ♣ K 5 3

d ♠ Q 9 8 6
   ♥ A K 5   *2D*
   ♦ Q J 7
   ♣ K 5 3

3. What is your next bid on each of these hands?

a
- ♠ 9 8 7 5 4
- ♥ 9 7 4
- ♦ 8 6 4 2
- ♣ 4

You	Partner
	2♣
2♦	2♥
?	

3 C

b
- ♠ K Q 8 2
- ♥ K 10 7 6
- ♦ Q 4
- ♣ J 8 5

You	Partner
	2♣
2♦	2NT
?	

3E

c
- ♠ 7 6 5 4
- ♥ Q 8 6 2
- ♦ 7 3
- ♣ J 9 5

You	Partner
	2♣
2♦	2♠
?	

4S

d
- ♠ K J 9 3 2
- ♥ K 7 4
- ♦ Q 6 2
- ♣ 9 5

You	Partner
	2♣
2♦	2♥
?	

3H

e
- ♠ K J 9
- ♥ A J 7
- ♦ A K
- ♣ K Q J 10 5

You	Partner
2♣	2♦
2NT	4NT
?	

6N

f
- ♠ A K Q J 10 8 4
- ♥ A
- ♦ K Q J 10
- ♣ 7

You	Partner
2♣	2♦
?	

3S

ANSWERS

1 **a** 2♣ You will rebid 2NT to show a balanced hand with 22-23 HCP.

b 2♣ Although you have only 17HCP, once you add your distributional points you have more than enough; you can just about make game in your own hand. You will be able to investigate slam, but stop in game if partner has nothing useful.

c 1♦ You have a nice hand, but if partner cannot respond to 1♦, it is unlikely you can make game.

d 2♣ You will rebid 3NT to show a balanced hand with 24-25 HCP.

e 1♦ Experience has shown that this works best on unbalanced hands with no strong suit. You are not likely to get passed out in 1♦

f 1♠ You won't get passed out here, and you'll get to bid both suits.

2 **a** 2♠ You have more than 8 points and a qualifying 5-card suit.

b 2♦ Much as you would like to, you cannot pass. 2♦ simply tells partner that you don't have a descriptive positive bid to make. Next round you'll use a cheaper minor bid if you can.

c 2♦ The spades aren't good enough to bid directly (only one top honor), but you'll get plenty of chances to bid them later.

d 2♦ How can you have a hand this good opposite a 2♣ opener? For now, you await events. Remember, if partner has a heart void, your hand may not be as good as it looks!

3 **a** 3♣ Second negative, telling partner what a terrible hand you have. Support hearts later.

b 3♣ Stayman. You intend to bid a slam, but right now you don't know whether it will be in hearts, spades, or notrump.

c 4♠ The picture bid. You have spade support and a poor hand.

d 3♥ The strongest bid you can make at this stage. Once hearts are agreed, you can explore slowly for the right level to play at.

e 6NT Partner's 4NT was quantitative, asking you to bid slam with a maximum. You have 22 points, but a good 5-card suit, so accept.

f 3♠ This was a trick question, since we did not discuss this earlier. Although 2♠ now is forcing to game, a jump below game tells partner that you have a solid suit, and want to play there even if he has a void. All you really need to know on this hand is how many aces partner has: but first tell him which suit is going to be trumps.

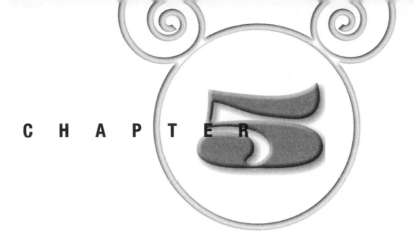

CHAPTER 5

REVERSES

WHAT'S IN A NAME?

♥ *Reverse* — adj. *Opposite or contrary in character or order.* A reverse is a sequence where opener rebids a suit at the two-level which is higher-ranking than his first-bid suit.

Look carefully at the following auctions:

A.
You	Partner
1♦	1♥
2♣	

B.
You	Partner
1♣	1♥
2♦ *(a reverse)*	

There is a subtle but vital difference between them: in sequence B, if partner simply wants to give preference to your first suit, he has to go to the three-level to do so. This is the fundamental definition of a **reverse**.

Normally, you would bid the higher-ranking of two equal-length suits first, so that you can get both suits in without getting too high. To reverse this order, and bid the lower suit first, you must have more length in your first suit, and better than a minimum hand.

Rules for reverses

1. ***A reverse is a sequence where partner has to go to the 3-level to give preference to opener's first suit.*** This occurs when opener (on his first rebid) bids a new suit at the two-level that is higher ranking than his first suit.

   Rule 1: A reverse shows at least 16 high-card points. The first-bid suit is always a longer suit than the second suit.

   Rule 2: A reverse promises an unbalanced hand — at least 5-4.

2. ***Use a reverse sequence only when your hand fits both these rules.***

3. ***Reverses are forcing one round — partner may not pass.***

Reversing says to your partner, 'I have a very good hand and my first suit is longer than my second'. Here's an example of a hand that would fit Sequence B:

♠ A 4   ♥ K 5   ♦ A J 8 4   ♣ K Q 10 9 5

With 5 clubs, 4 diamonds, and 17 high card points, this hand conforms to both rules and so qualifies for a reverse. Take away the ♠A, though, and the hand would no longer fit both rules, so could not be handled by reversing.

This hand also fits both rules (at least 17 points and at least 5-4 in two suits)

♠ K J 9 6   ♥ A K Q 6 3   ♦ A 8 5   ♣ 8

You	Partner
1♥	2♦
2♠	

What do you do with two-suiters too weak to reverse?

An opening bid of one of a suit has a very wide range, anything from a shapely 11-HCP hand up to a twenty-plus-point monster. Now 13-20 is an awfully wide range for one bid, so when it comes time to rebid you want to define your hand quickly and accurately. You also want to describe your shape, if possible. Balanced hands (no singletons or voids, no more than one doubleton) are described by opening or rebidding notrump. Unbalanced hands are a little more complex. With a minimum unbalanced hand (less than 16 points) you have only four options:

1. ***Rebid your own suit as cheaply as possible.***

♠ 6 4   ♥ K 5   ♦ A J 8 4   ♣ K Q 10 9 5

You	Partner
1♣	1♠
2♣	

You have the shape for a reverse, but not the HCP. Just rebid your five-card suit.

2.   *Make single raise in partner's suit.*

♠ K 6 4   ♥ 5   ♦ A Q J 4   ♣ Q 10 9 5 3

You	Partner
1♣	1♠
2♠	

Lacking the strength to bid 2♦, you can rebid clubs, or choose to raise partner.

> **BY THE WAY**
>
> *When you raise responder's major, you promise three to an honor (although you prefer to have four).*

3.   *Rebid a second suit at the two-level that is lower-ranking than your first suit.*

♠ K 6   ♥ 4 3   ♦ A Q J 5 4   ♣ Q 10 9 5

You	Partner
1♦	1♥
2♣	

This rebid does not promise anything extra — partner can go back to diamonds without going to the three-level.

4.   *Bid a new suit at the one-level.*

♠ K 6 5 4   ♥ 4   ♦ A Q J 5 4   ♣ Q 10 9

You	Partner
1♦	1♥
1♠	

Notice that here even though the second suit you bid is higher-ranking than the first, partner can still give you preference at the two-level. This sequence does not promise anything extra, therefore; it is *not* a reverse.

Should you reverse with a strong balanced hand?

The short answer to that question is 'No'. A reverse always shows an *unbalanced* hand. So while on hands like this:

♠ Q 7   ♥ K Q 8 5   ♦ A K 9 3   ♣ A J 4

You	Partner
1♦	1♠
?	

it may look right to reverse into 2♥ now, if you apply the rules you will realize that this hand doesn't fit Rule 2. In this case, you should rebid 2NT which shows 18-19 high-card points and a balanced hand. Doesn't that seem like an accurate description of this hand?

What do you do when partner reverses?

Partner	You
1♦	1♠
2♥	?

The first rule is that you *must* bid. Partner's reverse is forcing for one round, so even with a total dog you have to bid something. With a hand that doesn't want to play in game opposite 16-17 points) then you can do one of three things:

1. *Rebid your own suit at the minimum level.*
2. *Give preference to opener's first suit at the minimum level.*
3. *Bid notrump at the minimum level.*

Any of these show a very weak hand and opener is allowed to pass. Anything else you do creates a game-force: bidding must continue until game is reached.

If you originally responded at the two-level (showing 10+ points) and opener reverses (showing 16+) then you clearly have enough values between you for game, so this kind of sequence is automatically game-forcing.

Summary

✓ Opener reverses when he rebids a new suit at the two-level that is higher-ranking than his first suit.

✓ To make a reverse you must have 16+ points and more cards in your first suit than your second.

✓ You may never reverse on a balanced hand.

✓ A reverse is forcing — responder must keep the bidding alive for at least one round. After an initial two-level response, a reverse is forcing to game.

✓ With a weak hand facing a reverse, you can bid notrump or repeat any previously mentioned suit at the cheapest level. These bids are all non-forcing and opener can pass. Any other bid you make is game-forcing.

✓ With enough values to play in game opposite 16-17 points, you must make a forcing bid after partner reverses (unless you have already bid at the two-level).

REVERSES

NOW TRY THESE...

What is your next bid on each of these auctions?

1
- ♠ K Q 6
- ♥ A Q 10 7
- ♦ 7
- ♣ Q 10 8 6 4

You	Partner
1♣	1♠
?	

2
- ♠ A Q 6 4
- ♥ K 9 7 5 3 2
- ♦ K 4
- ♣ 5

You	Partner
1♥	1NT
?	

3
- ♠ K Q 6
- ♥ A Q 10 7
- ♦ 7
- ♣ Q 10 8 6 4

You	Partner
1♣	1♦
?	

4
- ♠ K Q 10 4
- ♥ A K Q 7 5 3
- ♦ —
- ♣ K J 3

You	Partner
1♥	1NT
?	

5
- ♠ K 6
- ♥ 7 3
- ♦ A Q 8 6
- ♣ A Q J 8 5

You	Partner
1♣	1♠
?	

6
- ♠ J 7 5 3 2
- ♥ J 5 3
- ♦ A 6
- ♣ 9 7 4

You	Partner
	1♣
1♠	2♦
?	

7
- ♠ K Q 10
- ♥ K 8 5 3
- ♦ J 6 3
- ♣ 10 8 6

You	Partner
	1♣
1♥	2♦
?	

8
- ♠ K 10
- ♥ K 8 5 4 3
- ♦ Q 6
- ♣ A 10 8 6

You	Partner
	1♣
1♥	2♦
?	

9
- ♠ 10 6
- ♥ K Q 8 5 4 3
- ♦ A 6 4
- ♣ 10 8

You	Partner
	1♣
1♥	2♦
?	

10
- ♠ 10 6
- ♥ K Q 8 5 4 3
- ♦ 10 6 4
- ♣ 10 8

You	Partner
	1♣
1♥	2♦
?	

ANSWERS

1	2♠	You are too weak to bid 2♥. Raising spades is preferable to rebidding your indifferent clubs.
2	2♥	You are not interested in game opposite a 1NT response, but this will likely be the best contract. You are too weak for 2♠, and besides, partner cannot have four spades on this auction.
3	1♥	Rebidding a second suit at the 1-level does not show extras.
4	2♠	This is forcing, so partner cannot pass. You don't intend to play in spades, but this is the best way to describe your hand. When you rebid hearts, partner will know you have a strong hand with 4-6 in the majors.
5	2♦	This hand is worth a reverse — just!
6	3♣	You are not interested in game if partner has only 16 or 17 points. Your spades are not worth rebidding, and your heart stopper is not good enough for 2NT. Note that even with three diamonds and only two clubs, 3♣ would be the right bid (opener has more clubs than diamonds).
7	3NT	Your hand is too good to bid only 2NT, which partner can pass. You have solid stoppers in the fourth suit (spades) so jump to what is the most likely game.
8	4♣	Time to tell partner about your club support, and if you bid only 3♣, partner could pass. Your ♦Q is a big card too, and slam is not out of the question.
9	3♥	It's not clear yet what the right game is. Make a forcing bid and keep describing your hand.
10	2♥	Notice the difference between this hand and the one in Question 9, and the way they are bid as a result. With any luck partner will pass this...

CHAPTER 6

BLACKWOOD and GERBER

WHAT'S IN A NAME?

Easley Blackwood (1903-1992) of Indianapolis invented his convention in 1933. He was a successful bridge teacher and writer, as well as a chess player and singer. The Blackwood convention is played in some form by just about every regular partnership in organized bridge. *John Gerber (1906-1981)* of Houston devised his convention in 1938.

The Blackwood convention uses a bid of 4NT to ask partner how many aces he has. Let's say you have the following hand:

♠ A K 8 6 4   ♥ K Q 9 6 2   ♦ 7   ♣ K Q

You	Partner
1♠	2♥
4NT (Blackwood)	

Do you really need to know anything other than how many aces partner holds? If he has two aces, you expect to make 6♥, and if he has all three missing aces then he will surely be able to make all thirteen tricks. In the event that he has only one, then you want to play in 4♥ or 5♥.

The beauty of Blackwood is its simplicity. To answer partner's question you show how many aces you have by bidding as follows:

5♣	=	0 aces or 4 aces
5♦	=	1 ace
5♥	=	2 aces
5♠	=	3 aces

We shall return later the question of how you tell whether partner has zero or four aces when he responds 5♣.

So when's a good time for Blackwood?

The simple answer to this question is 'When the only thing you need to know is how many aces partner holds'. That may seem obvious, but it is worth thinking about a little more. If you're going to make a small slam, you need a number of conditions to be true:

1. *You must be able to make twelve tricks.*

2. *You must have a sufficiently strong trump suit, or*

3. *If you are going to play in notrump, all suits must be adequately stopped.*

4. *The opponents must not be able to take two quick tricks.*

Let's look at each of these requirements in turn.

1. *You must be able to make twelve tricks.*

Partner	You
♠ A K 7	♠ Q J 3
♥ K 6 4	♥ A 8 5 2
♦ A 7 4 3	♦ K 8 6 2
♣ K J	♣ A Q

This is a rather extreme example, but it emphasizes the point. You have a combined 34 HCP including all of the aces and kings. Even so, there is no guarantee you can make any more than nine tricks, let alone twelve! However, using Blackwood will not tell you that you cannot make a slam on this hand.

2. *You must have a sufficiently strong trump suit.*

Partner	You
♠ A K 3	♠ Q J
♥ K 5 4 3	♥ A 7 5 2
♦ A 6 4	♦ K Q 5 3
♣ K Q 7	♣ J 8 3

Do you really want to play in 6♥ on this hand? Of course not — the defenders have the ♣A and a sure heart trick. Indeed, if trumps break particularly poorly, you might not even be able to make *game* in hearts! Using Blackwood would not tell you this, though.

3. **If you are going to play in notrump, all suits must be adequately stopped.**

Partner	You
♠ A 8 6	♠ 9 5 2
♥ K Q 7	♥ J 10 6 4
♦ A Q 6	♦ K J 2
♣ K J 7 3	♣ A Q 8

This time you can eventually make twelve tricks — one spade, three hearts, three diamonds and four clubs. However, assuming they lead a spade, the defenders will have established their two tricks before you will be able to cash your twelve. Since you have three of the four aces, Blackwood will not tell you that the six-level is too high on these cards either.

4. **The opponents must not be able to take two quick tricks.**

Partner	You
♠ K Q 7 3 2	♠ A J 8 5
♥ A K	♥ 5 3 2
♦ 5	♦ K Q 6 4
♣ K Q J 4 2	♣ 9 3

Now you have plenty of tricks and an adequately solid trump suit, but of course the defenders can take two aces before you can make your twelve tricks. Blackwood can tell you not to bid this slam. This would be a sensible auction:

Partner	You
1♠	3♠
4NT	5♦
5♠	pass

If partner has two aces, then you plan to bid 6♠. When he has only one, you know the defenders have two aces to cash and so you stop at the relative safety of the five-level.

The important point is this: *out of all the necessary conditions for slam, there is only one that Blackwood can help to confirm.*

Is 4NT always Blackwood?

Yes, unless partner has opened the bidding in notrump or his first rebid was notrump. You will remember from the discussion of Stayman that in both these auctions, for example, 4NT is a quantitative raise:

Partner	You
1NT	4NT

Partner	You
1NT	2♣
2♥	4NT

However, if the opening bid was in notrump, you can use the **Gerber** convention (a jump to 4♣) instead of Blackwood to ask for aces:

Partner	You	
1NT	4♣	(Gerber)

Partner	You	
1NT	2♣	
2♥	4♣	(Gerber)

Gerber and Blackwood responses follow similar principles. After 1NT-4♣:

4♦	=	0 or 4 aces
4♥	=	1 ace
4♠	=	2 aces
4NT	=	3 aces

Is there life after Blackwood?

Once you hear how many aces partner holds you will usually just pick the final contract. However, if you are interested in a grand slam you can continue with a bid of 5NT to ask partner how many kings he holds. Bidding 5NT to ask for kings *guarantees* that your side holds all of the aces and that you expect to make thirteen tricks if partner has an appropriate number of kings. The responses are identical to the first round but one level higher:

6♣	=	0 or 4 kings
6♦	=	1 king
6♥	=	2 kings
6♠	=	3 kings

BY THE WAY

Similarly, after a Gerber 4♣ bid and response, you can bid 5♣ to ask for kings. Again, the responses are identical to the first round, but one level higher.

You must also be able to handle any response partner makes to Blackwood when you decide to use it. When you intend to play in a minor suit, you must be especially careful. For example, if clubs is your suit and you hold only one ace yourself, then you cannot use Blackwood since a 5♦ response (showing one ace) would carry you too high. The exception to this rule is when you think you can play the hand in notrump as well as in a suit. Let's say your agreed suit is clubs. You bid 4NT holding one ace and partner bids 5♦ (showing one ace). There are two aces missing: what now? You cannot bid 5NT as that would ask for kings. However, a bid of 5♥ or 5♠ (because it is an unbid suit at the 5-level and thus cannot be natural) now asks partner to bid 5NT, which you intend to pass. Even with this neat little safety net available, before using Blackwood you must be sure that you have eleven tricks in notrump even though the opponents have two aces.

Let's not go that way...

Here's a potential problem to stay away from:

| ♠ AK864 | ♥ KQ962 | ♦ — | ♣ KQJ |

You	Partner
1♠	2♥
?	

This time you have a void, and that creates real problems if you use Blackwood. Suppose partner shows you one ace: if it's the ♦A, the most you will make is 5♥. If it's the ♥A or the ♣A, you want to be in 6♥. Similarly, if he has two aces, you still don't know whether to play in 6♥ or 7♥.

This kind of hand is also a problem:

| ♠ AK864 | ♥ KQ962 | ♦ 74 | ♣ K |

You	Partner
1♠	2♥
?	

Even if partner has two aces, you may be off two quick diamond tricks, so you can't be sure you want to be in slam. The answer is not to use Blackwood on hands which contain a void or two quick losers in an unbid suit. There are other, better ways to handle these situations which we'll deal with later in this book.

No aces, partner? None at all?

Earlier, we said we would return to the question of how you know whether partner has zero or four aces when he responds 5♣. This may seem like a potential problem, although in reality it never is. Say you bid 4 NT holding two aces. Partner responds 5♣. How many does he have — 0 or 4? Of course, he has zero.

If you have no aces and partner bids 5♣, then he must have all four or you are both bidding like maniacs. If you are bidding Blackwood, it is a reasonable assumption that you already know that between you and partner you have enough high card points to be interested in a slam. That hardly seems possible if neither of you has any aces.

Summary

✓ Unless the opening bid or opener's first rebid was in notrump, 4NT is almost always Blackwood.

✓ To respond to partner's 4NT, show your aces by bidding 5♣ with 0/4 aces, 5♦ with 1 ace, 5♥ with 2 aces, or 5♠ with 3 aces.

✓ Once you have used Blackwood, you may next bid 5NT to ask for kings. This guarantees that your side has all four aces, and that you expect to make thirteen tricks if partner has the appropriate number of kings. The responses to 5NT are similar to the responses to 4NT, but at the six-level.

✓ When the opening bid is in notrump, you can jump to 4♣ (Gerber) to ask for aces. Partner responds by bidding 4♦ with 0/4 aces, 4♥ with 1 ace, 4♠ with 2 aces, or 4NT with 3 aces. Once you have used Gerber, you may next bid 5♣ to ask for kings; the responses are similar, but one level higher.

✓ Before using Blackwood or Gerber, be sure that the only thing you need to know is how many aces partner holds.

✓ Do not use Blackwood or Gerber if you have a void, or if you have two quick losers in a suit, since the response will not tell you what you need to know.

BLACKWOOD AND GERBER

NOW TRY THESE...

What is your next bid on each of these hands?

1
♠ A K 10 8 6 5 3
♥ 4
♦ K Q J 7
♣ 5

You	Partner
1♠	3♠
?	

2
♠ A K 7 5 4
♥ 6
♦ K Q 8 5 2
♣ K Q

You	Partner
1♠	2♦
?	

3
♠ K 6
♥ A
♦ K Q 10 8 5 3
♣ K Q 6 3

You	Partner
	1♠
2♦	3♦
?	

4
♠ K Q 10 9 6 4
♥ A K Q
♦ K Q J
♣ A

You	Partner
2♣	2♦
2♠	3♠
?	

5
♠ K Q J 9 7 6 3
♥ 6
♦ A K J
♣ K 4

You	Partner
	1NT
?	

6
♠ A K Q
♥ A 9 7 5 2
♦ K Q 8 4
♣ 6

You	Partner
1♥	2♥
?	

7
♠ A K Q 7 5
♥ A J 6 4
♦ K Q 6
♣ A

You	Partner
2♣	2♥
?	

8
♠ K Q J 9 6 4
♥ A K 8 4
♦ —
♣ K 6 3

You	Partner
1♠	3♠
?	

9
♠ A K 10 7 5 3
♥ 8 4
♦ K Q J 5
♣ A

You	Partner
1♠	3♠
?	

10
♠ K J 4
♥ A 7 4
♦ K Q 10 5
♣ K 8 3

You	Partner
	1NT
?	

ANSWERS

1 **4NT** If partner has two aces you will bid 6♠. If he has only one ace you will sign off in 5♠. It is possible that partner has no aces, so using Blackwood even on this huge hand is not without risk.

2 **4NT** All you really need to know is how many aces partner has. If he has two aces, bid 6♦. If he has all three missing aces, bid the grand slam.

3 **4NT** As with Problem 2, knowing how many aces partner has will tell you how high to bid. No other information is relevant.

4 **4NT** Blackwood will tell you everything you need to know. If partner has an ace, bid 6♠, and if he has two, bid the grand slam.

5 **4♣** This is the Gerber convention, used opposite a strong notrump opening. If partner shows zero or one ace, sign off in 4♠. If he has two, bid 6♠, and if he has all three missing aces, bid 7♠.

6 **4♥** Partner might easily have an ace, but if he does then he is very unlikely to have both the king and queen of hearts. Your trump suit is not good enough to look for slam.

7 **3♥** You will recall that partner's 2♥ response to 2♣ guarantees at least two of the top three honors. As you have the ace, he must have at least ♥KQxxx, and thus all you need to know is whether he also has the missing ♦A. However, if you bid 4NT now, it would show a 28+ HCP balanced hand (see p. 43). So raise hearts now, then use Blackwood at your next turn.

8 **??** You cannot use Blackwood here, since the response will not help you. If partner shows an ace, it may be the ♦A or it may be one of the two useful aces: you can never find out. Exactly what you should bid now, we shall discuss in Chapter 14 on control-showing cuebids.

9 **??** This is the other type of hand on which players frequently misuse Blackwood. As with Question 8, knowing how many aces partner has doesn't solve your problem, and therefore Blackwood is the wrong tool. Say partner shows one ace: you still do not know whether the opponents have the ♥AK to cash. This problem is another that can be solved using cuebids (see Chapter 14).

10 **4NT** No, this is not Blackwood. Partner has opened 1NT and therefore 4♣ would ask for aces. This is a quantitative notrump raise, inviting partner to bid 6NT with a maximum or pass if he is minimum.

NEGATIVE DOUBLES

WHAT'S IN A NAME?

Negative Doubles in their modern form were introduced to tournament play by *Alvin Roth* of Boca Raton and *Tobias Stone* of New York City in 1957. They were known at the time as 'Sputnik' doubles, after the Russian space satellite of the same period. The idea, however, originated with *Lou Scharf* of New York in 1937.

The simplest situation where a negative double is used is an auction like this:

LHO	Partner	RHO	You
	1♦	1♠	dbl

Hands where you want to make a penalty double of a low-level overcall occur very infrequently. It is far more useful to use the double here to say to partner 'I have some points but no suitable bid'. When you make a negative double, you have enough points to respond to partner's opening bid had the opponent passed. You will also usually have four cards in each of the two unbid suits. You will always be able to stand partner's bidding any unbid major suit, and if you do not have the unbid minor you will have support for opener's suit. A typical hand for a negative double in the above auction would be:

♠ 7 4 2 ♥ K Q 7 3 ♦ Q 6 ♣ Q 9 7 2

You were about to bid 1♥ until the opponent stuck his nose into your auction, but the overcall has left you with no sensible bid. You can hardly support partner's diamonds on a doubleton, while bidding 1NT would promise a stopper in the enemy's spade suit. New major suits at the two-level show five-card suits and more high-card points than you have. You could pass, but then partner will never believe you have nine points and will not compete when it is right to do so. The **negative double** solves all these problems.

Think of a negative double as a takeout double by responder, showing support for the unbid suits. To make a negative double at the one-level you need at least 6 points (i.e. the values for a response had RHO passed), but you could have a very strong hand. Naturally, the higher the level at which you are forcing partner to respond to your double, the better hand you have to have — at least 10 if partner will have to bid at the three-level, and a full opening bid if you are forcing him even higher. How high you play negative doubles is up to you and your partner, but we recommend playing them up to and including overcalls of 3♠.

Negative doubles when there are two unbid majors

A negative double promises support for any unbid major — that means both of them if neither has been bid. This may sound restrictive, but there are times when the opponent's overcall will actually help you describe your hand better.

♠ A Q 7 5 ♥ J 8 4 2 ♦ 8 6 2 ♣ Q 4

If partner opens 1♣ and the next player passes, you normally bid your lower 4-card major (1♥) even though your spades are better. However, if RHO overcalls 1♦ then you have a chance to show both of your suits with one bid — a negative double. The overcall has, in effect, allowed you to bid One Spart (ie. 1♥ and 1♠ at the same time) in response to your partner's 1♣ opening!

If the auction starts 1♣-(1♦)-? there are two types of hand on which you will make a negative double. Any hand with 6+ points and exactly two four-card majors will start by making a negative double. You may have a hand something like the one above, or maybe one much stronger. If you have a stronger hand than the one above, the double will immediately tell partner that you have 4-4 in the majors. Then, having found a fit, you can decide to invite game, bid game, or even investigate a slam depending on the strength of your hand.

The second type of hand on which you will start with a negative double over 1♣-(1♦)-? has 5-4 (or 4-5) in the majors but is not strong enough to bid twice. To bid twice you need enough points to go to the three-level (10+). If you have:

♠ K 10 7 6 3 ♥ A 9 7 4 ♦ J 4 ♣ 8 2

then if you simply start with a natural 1♠, you are too weak to bid 2♥ (which would be forcing) over partner's 2♣ rebid — partner has to bid at least 3♥ if he prefers hearts to spades. However, making a negative double over the 1♦ overcall, instead, shows both majors with one bid. Once again, the opponent's overcall allows you to get both your suits into the game.

Warning: you must never lie about having both majors when you make a negative double. Consider this hand:

♠ J 4 ♥ K J 7 2 ♦ 5 3 ♣ A K Q 5 2

The auction starts:

LHO	Partner	RHO	You
			1♣
1♦	dbl	3♦	?

Trusting partner to have at least four hearts, you can afford to compete by bidding 3♥ here. You can see what a mess your side will be in if partner has decided to make a negative double with four spades and only three hearts. If you have only one four-card major and the bidding starts 1♣ - (1♦) - ? just bid your major — the bid you would have made had RHO passed partner's opening bid.

The other basic situation in which there will be two unbid majors is when partner opens 1♦ and RHO overcalls 2♣. The requirements for making a negative double in this auction are identical to those discussed above except that with only 4-4 in the majors you should have 8+ points.

Doubling a 1♥ overcall

LHO	Partner	RHO	You
			1♣
1♥	dbl		

This auction is worth thinking about. There is only one unbid major, and partner had room to bid it at the one-level. So what is the difference between a negative double here and a 1♠ bid?

We recommend that you use the negative double to promise exactly four spades, so that if partner bids 1♠ here you know he has at least five of them. This is the kind of situation where this agreement can be very useful:

♠ Q 10 5 ♥ A 7 ♦ J 4 2 ♣ A Q 8 5 3

LHO	Partner	RHO	You
			1♣
1♥	1♠	2♥	?

Do you raise partner's spades? The answer is that you want to compete to 2♠ if partner has:

♠ K J 7 4 2 ♥ 8 3 ♦ A 9 5 3 ♣ J 7

but not if he has:

♠ K 7 4 2 ♥ 8 5 3 ♦ A 9 5 3 ♣ J 7

BY THE WAY

When partner opens a minor, and RHO overcalls 1♥, not everyone plays that a 1♠ bid by responder shows 5+ spades, and a negative double exactly four. We recommend it here because it's useful and easy to remember.

Knowing partner has at least five spades, you can raise him with confidence. Of course, you might get away with a 2♠ bid on this hand even if partner has only a four-card suit, but consider the problem if overcaller's partner can jump the bidding to the three-level:

♠ Q 10 5   ♥ 7   ♦ K Q 4 2   ♣ A K 8 5 3

LHO	Partner	RHO	You
			1♣
1♥	1♠	3♥	?

You are not happy bidding 3♠ if partner might have only four spades. Bidding or passing could both be disastrous.

Doubling to show four hearts

At the very start of this chapter, you saw how a negative double of a 1♠ overcall showed (or strongly implied) a four-card heart suit. Responder might still have a very strong hand when making a negative double after 1♣-(1♦), and the same is true in the auctions 1♣-(1♠)-dbl and 1♦-(1♠)-dbl. All balanced hands of 6+ points with four hearts must start by making a negative double. However, since a negative double is unlimited, you might have much more than six points. Discover if you have a heart fit first, and then decide how high you want to bid.

What if both majors have been bid?

If the auction starts 1♥-(1♠)-? or 1♠-(2♥)-? a negative double from responder shows both minors. Obviously, you must have more high-card values (10+ is a good guide) to double after the second auction since opener must go to the three-level in order to bid one of your suits.

Bidding versus doubling at the two-level

If the opponents have left you room to bid at the one-level, you can use your normal bids as well as a negative double. However, if partner opens 1♦ and RHO overcalls 1♠, you have less room to maneuver. If you have five or more hearts, for example, you want to introduce your suit but how you do so will depend on the strength of your hand.

♠ 5   ♥ A Q 10 7 4   ♦ K 5 4   ♣ J 8 5 3

LHO	Partner	RHO	You
	1♦	1♠	?

If you have 10+ points (including distribution) then you can bid 2♥. This is forcing, so partner must bid again, even with a minimum opening. This is the minimum sort of hand you should have for a forcing bid at the two-level.

So, what do you do with a weaker hand? Let's say something like:

♠ 5 ♥ Q 10 9 6 4 2 ♦ K 6 ♣ J 8 5 3

LHO	Partner	RHO	You
	1♦	1♠	dbl
pass	2♦	pass	2♥
all pass			

Despite the extra heart, this hand is simply not good enough for a forcing 2♥ bid. That is not to say that you have to pass though. Instead, you can start with a negative double and then bid 2♥ on the next round of bidding. Partner is now allowed to pass 2♥.

How do you deal with a jump overcall?

The negative double can be especially useful when the opponents make a pre-emptive jump overcall.

♠ 9 5 ♥ K J 9 2 ♦ 10 9 5 ♣ A Q 9 3

LHO	Partner	RHO	You
	1♦	2♠	?

You cannot bid 3♣ or 3♥ since bidding any new suit at the three-level promises at least five cards in that suit. How much easier life would be if you could make two bids in one — a bid showing both unbid suits and enough high-card values to compete to at least the three-level would be ideal, wouldn't it? Aren't you glad that you agreed to play negative doubles, for that is exactly what the bid shows.

If you decide to play negative doubles of overcalls through 3♠, as was suggested earlier, then you must remember that the higher the overcall the more values you need to double. If the bidding starts 1♣-(1♥)-? you can make a negative double to show your four-card spade suit on either of these two hands:

♠ K 8 7 3 ♥ 6 4 ♦ K J 6 3 ♣ J 5 2

♠ A Q 8 3 ♥ A 4 ♦ K J 6 3 ♣ J 5 2

However, if the bidding starts 1♣-(3♥)-? you have to pass with the first hand. You do not have enough high-card points to force partner to bid at the three- or four-level if he has only a minimum opening bid. Of course, with the second hand you are planning to bid game anyway, but you make a negative double to show your spade suit first. Eventually you will play game or slam in spades, clubs, notrump or even diamonds.

The higher the overcall, the more points you must have to bid or double. If partner is able to bid either of the suits you have promised at the two-level, then you can have as little as 6+ points. If you force partner to the three-level (e.g.

1♦- (2♠)-dbl) then you need at least 10 points. If the overcall is above three of partner's original suit (1♦-(3♥)-dbl) then you must have an opening bid to make a negative double. However, if you have good support for partner's suit and/or compensating distributional values, then you can reduce the high-card requirements a little in all these cases.

What do you do when partner makes a negative double?

Remember the idea that a negative double is a takeout double by responder — it generally shows interest in the unbid suits. So with four-card support for one of the suits partner has shown by doubling, you bid that suit. Your first choice is always to bid an unbid major if you have four of them. Without four cards in an unbid major, you can bid notrump (with a stopper in the opponent's suit) or rebid your original suit. With a minimum opening bid (up to 15 points) you bid as cheaply as possible. With 16-17 points you can jump in one of partner's suits or in notrump. With 18-19 points you can bid game (just as you would opposite a natural response to your opening bid).

Let us go back to the hand we saw at the very start of this chapter and see how some complete auctions might go:

Partner	You
♠ 7 4 2	♠ J 5
♥ K Q 7 3	♥ A J 6 2
♦ Q 6	♦ K 9 5 3 2
♣ Q 9 7 2	♣ K 8

LHO	Partner	RHO	You
			1♦
1♠	dbl	pass	2♥
all pass			

With a minimum opener, you support partner's hearts at the lowest possible level; partner will pass.

Partner	You
♠ 7 4 2	♠ J 4
♥ K Q 7 3	♥ A J 6 2
♦ Q 6	♦ A K 5 3 2
♣ Q 9 7 2	♣ K J

LHO	Partner	RHO	You
			1♦
1♠	dbl	pass	3♥
pass	4♥	all pass	

On this hand, in contrast, you have enough to jump to 3♥, inviting partner to go on to game. With 9 HCP, and the ♦Q likely to be useful, he will bid game.

	Partner		You
	♠ 7 4 2		♠ A J 6 2
	♥ K Q 7 3		♥ J
	♦ Q 6		♦ A K 5 3 2
	♣ Q 0 7 2		♣ K J 4

LHO	Partner	RHO	You
			1♦
1♠	dbl	pass	2NT
pass	3NT	all pass	

Again you have values for a game invitation, but this time no fit for partner. 2NT describes your values, and lets partner know you have spades well under control. With that assurance, partner can again accept the game try by bidding 3NT.

Can you still double the opponents for penalties?

Not only can you still catch the opponents for a penalty when responder has a trump stack, but there will even be times when you can collect a penalty that you would have missed if you were playing standard penalty doubles. Let's say you have:

♠ A Q 10 8 7   ♥ 8   ♦ 9 6 3   ♣ A J 8 4

Partner opens 1♦ and RHO overcalls 1♠! You would like to defend 1♠ doubled but you are playing negative doubles. What can you do? Must you let the opponents escape? Not at all — just pass! This is called a *trap pass*.

Playing negative doubles, opener is expected to bid again most of the time if LHO overcalls and that is followed by two passes. Usually, he will reopen with a double, allowing responder to pass for penalties when he has a hand such as the one above. The only time opener is allowed to pass is when he has a minimum hand and length in the opponent's suit, thus making it clear that responder cannot have made a trap pass. On this hand, when partner reopens with a double, you can happily pass and convert it to a penalty double.

NEGATIVE DOUBLES

✓ When partner opens one of a suit, and RHO overcalls in a suit, a double by you is negative. If partner opens 1NT, or RHO bids 1NT over partner's one-of-a-suit opening, double by you is for penalties.

✓ To make a negative double at the one-level you need 6+ points (i.e. the values for a response had RHO passed).

✓ The higher the overcall, the more high-card strength you need to make a negative double.

✓ A negative double always guarantees support for any unbid major. If you do not have support for an unbid minor then you will have a fit for partner's suit.

✓ To make a negative double when there are two unbid major suits, you must have at least four cards in both majors.

✓ When partner opens a minor and the opponent overcalls 1♥, a negative double shows exactly four spades and a 1♠ bid shows at least a five-card suit.

✓ If you bid a new major suit at the two-level over the overcall, you must have at least a five-card suit and 10+ points. With a five-card or longer major suit but insufficient values to make a forcing bid in your suit, start with a negative double and then bid your suit over partner's response. This bid is now non-forcing.

✓ When partner makes a negative double, you should bid one of the unbid suits whenever you have a four-card suit. If you have a minimum opening bid, you make your bid at the lowest level available. With extra values, you may jump.

✓ If the overcall of your opening bid is followed by two passes, you should reopen with a double unless you have a minimum hand and length in the opponents' suit

NEGATIVE DOUBLES

NOW TRY THESE...

What is your next bid on each of these auctions?

1
- ♠ K J 6 3
- ♥ Q 10 5 2
- ♦ Q 5
- ♣ 7 4 3

LHO	Partner	RHO	You
	1♣	1♦	?

2
- ♠ K J 6 3
- ♥ Q 10 5
- ♦ Q 5 4 2
- ♣ 7 4

LHO	Partner	RHO	You
	1♣	1♦	?

3
- ♠ K J 9 6 3
- ♥ Q 10 5
- ♦ Q 2
- ♣ 7 5 4

LHO	Partner	RHO	You
	1♣	1♥	?

4
- ♠ K J 9 3
- ♥ Q 10 5
- ♦ Q J 8 2
- ♣ 7 5

LHO	Partner	RHO	You
	1♣	1♥	?

5
- ♠ K J 9 3
- ♥ J 10 5
- ♦ Q J 8 2
- ♣ 7 5

LHO	Partner	RHO	You
	1♣	3♥	?

6
- ♠ K J 9 7
- ♥ K J 10 5
- ♦ K 3 2
- ♣ A 5

LHO	Partner	RHO	You
	1♣	2♦	?

7
- ♠ 7 3
- ♥ K J 9 5
- ♦ A Q 8 2
- ♣ 7 6 5

LHO	Partner	RHO	You
	1♦	2♠	?

8
- ♠ 9 3
- ♥ A Q 8 6 5
- ♦ J 8 2
- ♣ A Q 5

LHO	Partner	RHO	You
	1♦	1♠	?

9
- ♠ K J 9 3
- ♥ 10 5
- ♦ A Q J 8 2
- ♣ Q 5

LHO	Partner	RHO	You
			1♦
1♠	dbl	pass	?

10
- ♠ K J 9 3
- ♥ 10 5
- ♦ A K J 8 2
- ♣ K 5

LHO	Partner	RHO	You
			1♦
1♥	1♠	pass	?

11
- ♠ K J 9
- ♥ 10 5 3
- ♦ A Q J 8 2
- ♣ Q 5

LHO	Partner	RHO	You
			1♦
2♣	dbl	pass	2♦
pass	2♥	pass	?

12
- ♠ K J 9 3
- ♥ 10 5
- ♦ A Q J 8 2
- ♣ Q 5

LHO	Partner	RHO	You
			1♦
1♥	dbl	2♥	?

ANSWERS

1   dbl   You have two four-card majors and more than the necessary 6 points.

2   1♠   Double here would promise both majors.

3   1♠   This shows more than 6 points and at least five spades.

4   dbl   You have exactly four spades, more than the necessary 6 points, and both unbid suits.

5   pass   You have both unbid suits but not enough strength to force partner to bid at the three-level.

6   dbl   You have two unbid four-card majors. You can show your extra high-card strength on the next round.

7   dbl   You do have the unbid major, and although you don't have clubs, you have good support for partner's diamonds. If partner bids 3♣, you will retreat to 3♦. This says you have four hearts, but that you were just kidding about clubs.

8   2♥   You have an opening bid and a good five-card suit: more than enough to make a forcing bid.

9   1NT   A minimum notrump rebid: you have a spade stopper, and partner has promised hearts. Don't even think about passing for penalties — your spades are badly placed for defense.

10   3♠   This time all your high cards seem to be working well, and you have just discovered a nine-card trump fit (partner must have five spades).

11   pass   This is how partner shows you five or six hearts with too weak a hand to bid 2♥ directly over the 2♣ overcall.

12   2♠   Partner's double showed four spades.

C H A P T E R

JACOBY and TEXAS TRANSFERS

Using this convention, when partner opens 1NT and your RHO passes, the bids
of 2♦ and 2♥ each show at least five cards in the next suit *above* the one you have
actually bid. If you bid 2♦ (showing hearts) partner is expected to bid 2♥. If you
show spades with a 2♥ bid, then partner's next bid should be 2♠. These transfers at the two-level are called **Jacoby Transfers**.

Partner	You	
1NT	2♦	*(transfer to hearts)*
2♥		

Partner	You	
1NT	2♥	*(transfer to spades)*
2♠		

BY THE WAY

In club and tournament play, if your partner uses a transfer bid, you are required to alert the opponents at the time by saying 'Transfer' out loud.

In their simplest form, transfers do exactly what their name suggests — they transfer declaration of the hand from responder to opener. There are two main reasons why this is useful:

1. **The strong hand is concealed from the opponents** as the opening bidder becomes declarer and the weak hand is on view in dummy. This makes it harder for the opponents to defend accurately.

2. **The opening lead comes up to the strong hand**, and declarer will often gain an extra trick as a result.

When do you use a transfer?

Whenever you have a five-card or longer major-suit. *There are no other requirements.* That's right — no other requirements. You can make the same bid with three points and with twenty points. If that seems a little confusing, consider the major difference between these two auctions.

LHO	Partner	RHO	You
	1NT	pass	2♠[1]
pass	pass	pass	

1. Weak 'drop-dead' bid showing 5+ spades (not playing transfers)

LHO	Partner	RHO	You
	1NT	pass	2♥[1]
pass	2♠	pass	

1. Transfer to spades

You will notice that in the first auction (not playing transfers) you tell partner that you have five spades but by the time the bidding gets back around to you, the auction is over. In the second auction, you again tell partner about your spade suit, but this time you get to bid again if you wish. Of course, if you have a very weak hand, you will pass now and the contract will be the same. However, you can also decide to bid on if you have more points.

How do you respond to a transfer?

You open 1NT and partner, for example, bids 2♦. What do you do? On the vast majority of hands you will simply bid 2♥ — partner's major. This is called completing the transfer. It says virtually nothing about your hand. There is only one exception: when you have four-card support, a ruffing value (i.e. not 3-4-3-3 shape) and a maximum for your 1NT, you should jump to 3♥. The reason for this is that, opposite a five-card or longer heart suit, if you revalue your hand in support of hearts you will find that it is now too strong for your 1NT opening. For example:

♠ K6　♥ KQ73　♦ AQ82　♣ QJ4

When you first pick up this hand as dealer you count it as 17 points. However, if partner were the dealer and opened 1♥ you would add distributional points to your high card values, making the hand worth more than 17 points.

What happens after partner completes your transfer?

In simple terms, you continue to bid your hand naturally. With a weak hand, you pass. With a balanced hand, and only a five-card major suit, you bid either 2NT or 3NT, depending on your hand strength. If partner has three-card support for your suit, he will correct to your suit at the right level. You may not rebid a five-card major suit — you have already told partner that you have five. Let's look at some examples:

♠ AQ532　♥ 93　♦ KJ4　♣ 974

Partner	You
1NT	2♥
2♠	3NT

You have enough for game, so you offer partner a choice between spades and notrump. If partner has three or more spades he will correct to 4♠. If he has only a doubleton spade he will pass 3NT.

Without transfers you would have jumped to 3♠ over 1NT with this hand, and again partner would have bid 3NT or 4♠ depending on how many spades he held. Two benefits of playing transfers are illustrated by this hand. First, the strong hand becomes declarer. More important, though, is the inference that when you jump directly to 3♥ or 3♠ over partner's 1NT opening you have a genuine slam try; partner will bid accordingly. Let's make your hand a little weaker:

♠ A5　♥ K9742　♦ 94　♣ J1053

Partner	You
1NT	2♦
2♥	2NT

This sequence tells partner both that you have enough to play in game if he has a maximum 1NT opening and that you have a five-card heart suit. This time, opener has four options. If he has a maximum 1NT, he will bid 3NT or 4♥

(depending on how many hearts he has). With a minimum, he will pass 2NT with a doubleton heart or correct to 3♥ with three-card support.

What about very strong balanced hands?

If you have enough to make a slam try with a relatively balanced hand containing a five-card major, you can transfer at the two-level and then bid 4NT:

Partner	You
1NT	2♥
2♠	4NT

This 4NT is not Blackwood: it has the same quantitative meaning as it does when you bid it directly over the 1NT opening except that now you have shown your five-card major. Obviously, instead of simply choosing between 4NT and 6NT, opener must now also consider 5♠ and 6♠ too.

If you are even stronger than this — a five-card major and the values to raise to 6NT — you transfer to your major at the two-level and bid 5NT.

Partner	You
1NT	2♥
2♠	5NT

This is *forcing* — opener must choose between 6NT and slam in your major.

What if you don't have a balanced hand?

Another common type of hand is one with invitational values and a six-card major. In this case, you are not really interested in playing notrump, but you do need to ask partner if he is minimum or maximum for his 1NT opening.

♠ A 4   ♥ Q J 10 7 5 3   ♦ 8 2   ♣ 9 8 6

Partner	You
1NT	2♦
2♥	3♥

You deal with this case by transferring, then raising to the three-level. If partner has a maximum, he will go on to 4♥; if not, he will pass. Notice that now you're not asking partner whether or not he likes hearts. You have six of them and he must have at least two for his 1NT opening. The only question you are asking is, 'Are you maximum for your 1NT?'; partner can choose only between playing 3♥ and 4♥.

Transfers are also useful to show very distributional, strong hands opposite partner's 1NT opening. Let's say you have

♠ K Q 6 4 2   ♥ A 3   ♦ 8   ♣ A 10 8 7 5

Partner	You
1NT	2♥
2♠	3♣

You have plenty of points for game, but it is easy to construct normal 1NT openings opposite which any of 3NT, 4♠, 5♣ or even 6♣ or 6♠ could be the right contract.

Playing transfers, you are able to show both your suits and still stay below 3NT in case that's the right place to play. When you transfer and then bid a new suit, it is forcing to game. You will usually be at least 5-5 in your two suits, but with more high-card strength you can be 5-4. You must always have a five-card major, though. Either way, partner should raise your second suit if he has four-card support.

There is no telling how the auction might continue on this hand, but it is only when playing transfers that you will be able to investigate all of the slam possibilities while staying at a safe enough level to stop in the right game if partner has the wrong hand.

What about strong major-suit hands?

If you have a six-card or longer major suit, and simply want to play game in your major, you still use transfers, but at the four-level rather than the two-level. These are called **Texas Transfers**.

Partner	You	
1NT	4♦	*(transfer to hearts)*

Partner	You	
1NT	4♥	*(transfer to spades)*

Partner has no choice in his first response here: he must simply complete the transfer. With only game-going values, you pass, and your partnership has arrived. If you want to explore slam possibilities, though, you can bid 4NT to ask for aces now — this time it *is* Blackwood!

Partner	You
1NT	4♦
4♥	4NT

Your Texas Transfer has *set the suit as hearts,* so 4NT is no longer quantitative, despite the fact that partner opened 1NT. Contrast this with the auction where you began with a Jacoby Transfer at the two-level.

JACOBY and TEXAS TRANSFERS

Summary

✓ Over partner's 1NT opening, 2♦ and 2♥ are transfers to hearts and spades respectively. Transfer whenever you have a five-card or longer major suit.

✓ Opener normally just completes the transfer. With a super-maximum and a good fit he may jump to the three-level in responder's suit over a Jacoby Transfer.

✓ With fewer than 8 points, and a five-card major, transfer at the two-level and then pass when it is next your turn to bid.

✓ With a five-card major and a balanced hand, transfer at the two-level and then rebid notrump at a level appropriate to your strength: 2NT= 8-9; 3NT= 10-15; 4NT=16-17; 5NT = 18+.

✓ When responder rebids notrump, opener should correct to responder's major with three-card support (or better), and also accept or reject any game or slam invitation.

✓ A transfer followed by the bid of a new suit is game-forcing. It shows at least 5-5 in the two suits, or 5-4 with slam interest.

✓ With a six-card or longer major and invitational values, transfer at the two-level and then invite by bidding your suit again at the three-level.

✓ With a six-card or longer major and values for game but no slam interest (8-13 HCP), use a Texas Transfer (4♦ or 4♥).

✓ With 15+ HCP and a six-card or longer major, normally start with direct jump to the three-level in your major. However, if all you need to know is how many aces partner has, you can transfer at the four-level and continue with Blackwood 4NT.

JACOBY AND TEXAS TRANSFERS

NOW TRY THESE...

1. On each of these hands, partner opens 1NT (15-17 points). What is your first bid? If you use a transfer, what do you plan to bid on the next round?

a
- ♠ A 8 6 4 2
- ♥ 7 6
- ♦ 9 6 5 2
- ♣ 3 2

b
- ♠ 9 7 6 4 3 2
- ♥ 4
- ♦ J 8 7 5
- ♣ Q 7

c
- ♠ K J 8 5 3
- ♥ Q 7
- ♦ Q 10 5
- ♣ 8 7 4

d
- ♠ A Q 7 5 3
- ♥ K J 7 5 3
- ♦ A 5
- ♣ 3

e
- ♠ A Q 7 5 3
- ♥ K J 5
- ♦ J 7 3
- ♣ 8 4

f
- ♠ A Q 7 5 3
- ♥ K J 6 3
- ♦ J 7
- ♣ 8 4

g
- ♠ J 10 8 6 3 2
- ♥ 4
- ♦ A 6 4 3
- ♣ Q 6

h
- ♠ Q J 8 6 4 3 2
- ♥ 8 5
- ♦ A 6
- ♣ Q 7

i
- ♠ J 9 7 5 3
- ♥ 8 6 4 3
- ♦ Q 4
- ♣ 9 3

j
- ♠ A Q J 7 6 4
- ♥ K 5
- ♦ 7 4
- ♣ K Q 5

2. What is your next bid on each of these hands?

a
- ♠ K Q 5
- ♥ A 5
- ♦ K J 7 3
- ♣ Q 10 9 5

You	Partner
1NT	2♥
2♠	2NT
?	

b
- ♠ K Q 5
- ♥ A 5
- ♦ K J 7 3
- ♣ Q 10 9 5

You	Partner
1NT	2♥
2♠	3♣
?	

c
- ♠ K Q 5
- ♥ A 5
- ♦ K J 7 3
- ♣ Q 10 9 5

You	Partner
1NT	2♦
2♥	3NT
?	

d
- ♠ K Q 5
- ♥ A 5
- ♦ K J 7 3
- ♣ Q 10 9 5

You	Partner
1NT	2♥
2♠	3NT
?	

ANSWERS

1 **a** 2♥ You will pass partner's 2♠.

  b 2♥ You will pass partner's 2♠. Despite the six-card suit you do not have enough to invite game.

  c 2♥ You will bid 2NT over partner's 2♠. You want to invite game and show your five-card spade suit. Opener will now choose the final contract — either 2NT, 3NT, 3♠ or 4♠.

  d 2♥ You will bid 3♥ over partner's 2♠. This tells partner that you have five or more spades along with five hearts and enough values for game.

  e 2♥ You will bid 3NT over partner's 2♠. This tells opener to choose between 3NT (if he has only two spades) and 4♠.

  f 2♣ Remember that you use Stayman with 5-4 in the majors and 8+ points.

  g 2♥ You will bid 3♠ over partner's 2♠. This invites opener to bid 4♠ with a maximum 1NT. With a minimum he will pass 3♠.

  h 4♥ You are not interested in slam, but you have enough for game and you want spades to be trumps. You will pass when partner completes the transfer with a 4♠ bid.

  i 2♥ You will pass partner's 2♠. Remember that to use Stayman on a weak hand you must be able to deal with any of the three possible responses. If partner responds 2♦ to Stayman here you will not then be able to bid 2♠ as that shows an invitational hand.

  j 3♠ This tells partner you have a good spade suit and interest in slam. Note that you should not transfer at the four-level and then use Blackwood because you have two losing diamonds; even if you have only have one ace missing the opponents may still be able to take the first two tricks.

2 **a** 3♠ With a minimum hand, you are declining the game invitation. However, with three-card support you should convert to partner's suit.

  b 4♣ Partner has a strong hand with black suits; your first duty is to raise clubs with four of them. Later you can support spades too.

  c pass With only a doubleton heart, you should choose to play the hand in notrump.

  d 4♠ Convert to spades with three-card support.

2

MORE
COMPLICATED

CHAPTER 9

JACOBY 2NT
FORCING MAJOR RAISE

WHAT'S IN A NAME?

♥ The Jacoby 2NT convention is another invention of the late great **Oswald Jacoby** *(1902-1984)* of Dallas, Texas, who also popularized transfer bids and weak jump overcalls.

Perhaps, when you first learned to play, you were taught that raising partner's major-suit opening to the three-level was forcing, showing trump support and 13-15 points. Some people still play that way. The problem with that, of course, is that you are rather stuck when you have one of those awkward invitational hands with four-card trump support for partner and 10-12 points (including distribution). You are too good for a simple raise to the two-level, but not good enough to insist on game. The modern style is to use the sequences 1♥-3♥ and 1♠-3♠ to show a 'limit raise' — an invitational hand.

When you adopt limit raises, you obviously cannot also use the raise to the three-level to show a game-going hand, possibly even with slam interest, so you have to find another way to do that. Jacoby's answer was to use 2NT for that purpose. Using 2NT rather than 3♥ or 3♠ for this purpose also keeps the bidding lower, enabling the opener to provide some useful information.

BY THE WAY

While using Jacoby 2NT shows a minimum of 13 points, the bid is actually unlimited. The 2NT bidder could in fact have a very strong hand.

How do you respond to Jacoby 2NT?

You can have three basic types of hand for a 1♥ or 1♠ opening:

1) an unbalanced hand with a singleton or void somewhere

2) a hand with a strong second five-card suit

3) a balanced or semi-balanced hand

Let's take each type of hand in turn. Let's say you have opened 1♥ in each case:

Type 1) An unbalanced hand with a singleton or void somewhere

♠ K 5 3   ♥ K Q J 6 3   ♦ 6   ♣ A J 5 2

Partner	You
	1♥
2NT	3♦

After partner has responded with 2NT (showing a game raise in hearts) you simply bid your singleton or void at the 3-level — in this case, 3♦. This says nothing about your strength, but simply tells partner that you have a singleton (or void) in the bid suit. To see how useful this information is, let's look at a couple of hands partner might have for his Jacoby 2NT bid:

Partner	You
♠ A 2	♠ K 5 3
♥ A 10 9 4	♥ K Q J 6 3
♦ 9 7 4 3	♦ 6
♣ K Q 4	♣ A J 5 2

Opposite a 1♥ opening, partner has a textbook game raise, and duly responds 2NT. Looking at the two hands together, you would certainly like to reach 6♥.

BY THE WAY

It is nearly always bad to have high cards in a suit where partner has a singleton or void. These are called 'wasted values'.

Partner	You
♠ A 2	♠ K 5 3
♥ A 10 9 4	♥ K Q J 6 3
♦ K Q 4	♦ 6
♣ 9 7 4 3	♣ A J 5 2

However, while his hand is equally strong this time too, if you look at the two hands you'll see that game is quite high enough. The difference, of course, is that in the second case the ♦KQ are wasted opposite opener's shortness, whereas in the first pair of hands all of your high cards are working.

Playing Jacoby 2NT these are simple hands to bid. Your 3♦ immediately tells partner that you have diamond shortness and he is well-placed to judge how well your hands fit. In the first case, he'll push onwards, knowing that you have no wasted values. In the second, he'll sign off in game, warned that there is serious diamond wastage.

BY THE WAY

What about those balanced 13-15 hands on which you used to bid a natural 2NT? For example, partner opens 1♠ and you have:
♠ 94 ♥ AJ4 ♦ AQ84 ♣ K983
Start by bidding your lowest suit (in this case, 2♣) and then bid the appropriate number of notrump at your second turn.

Type 2) A hand with a strong second five-card suit

♠ 8   ♥ K Q 10 8 7 3   ♦ 5   ♣ A Q 10 8 3

Partner	You
	1♥
2NT	4♣

If the auction starts 1♥-2NT, on this hand you jump to the four-level in your second suit. This does *not* deny a singleton or void — in fact, you're certain to have one. It does, however, emphasize that the most important feature of your hand is a good second suit. It is easy to construct forcing heart raises that fit well with this hand, and others that do not. By describing your hand immediately, you allow your partner to judge how well the hands fit together.

Partner	You
♠ A J 5	♠ 8
♥ A 10 9 4	♥ K Q 10 8 7 3
♦ 9 7 4 3	♦ 5
♣ K 4	♣ A Q 10 8 3

On this hand, partner knows that the ♣K is a magic card, and will press on to an excellent slam. With the ♦K instead of the ♣K, partner would be much more wary (you must be short in spades and diamonds, since you have two other 5-card suits); in fact, slam would be worse than 50% if his minors were reversed.

Type 3) A balanced or semi-balanced hand

♠ 9 8   ♥ K Q 10 8 7   ♦ Q 5   ♣ A J 10 3

Partner	You
	1♥
2NT	4♥

This type of hand has no singletons or voids — likely shapes are 5332, 5422 or 6322. However, there are three rebids available to describe these hands — 3♥, 3NT and 4♥. (Note that having found at least a 5-4 major-suit fit, you never want to play in 3NT and thus it can be given a conventional meaning.)

The most efficient method is that a jump to game (4♥ in the auction above) shows a completely minimum hand. (The logic of this is that partner has forced to game already, and with good hands we want to leave the maximum amount of room to explore slam. Getting to game immediately therefore shows the worst hand.) On the hand shown, this would be the appropriate response: it is a minimum opener, with no shortness, and semi-balanced.

There are, as usual, a number of variations and styles as to how to play the

BY THE WAY

2NT by responder is no longer Jacoby if the opponents overcall partner's major-suit opening bid. It reverts to its natural meaning.

3♥ rebid by opener, and what to use a rebid of 3NT to mean. We suggest you use 3♥ to show a better than minimum hand with very good trumps (two of the top three honors), and 3NT as better than minimum without very good trumps.

♠ A 8   ♥ K Q 10 8 7   ♦ Q 5   ♣ A J 10 3

Partner	You
	1♥
2NT	3♥

This hand certainly qualifies as better than minimum, and the trumps are good enough to make a 3♥ response.

♠ A 8   ♥ Q 10 8 7 4   ♦ Q 5   ♣ A K J 10

Partner	You
	1♥
2NT	3NT

This time, with poor trumps, rebid 3NT. Partner may even decide to play there!

Summary

✓ To use Jacoby 2NT over a 1♥ or 1♠ opener you must have:
    1) Game-forcing or better values
        AND
    2) At least four-card support for partner's major

✓ After partner uses Jacoby 2NT, you can rebid as follows:
    1) bid a suit at the three-level in which you are singleton or void
    2) jump to the four-level with a strong two-suiter
    3) with no singleton or void:
        — bid game in the agreed major with a minimum
        — bid three of the agreed major with extra values and
           good trumps (two of the top three honors)
        — rebid 3NT with extra values but poor trumps

JACOBY 2NT FORCING MAJOR RAISE

NOW TRY THESE...

What is your next bid on each of these hands?

1
- ♠ K J 6 3
- ♥ A 8
- ♦ A J 9 4
- ♣ 8 5 3

Partner	You
1♠	?

2
- ♠ A Q 9 4
- ♥ A 6
- ♦ A 9 5 4
- ♣ A K J

Partner	You
1♠	?

3
- ♠ A 7
- ♥ K Q 7
- ♦ J 10 8 3
- ♣ K J 10 7

Partner	You
1♠	?

4
- ♠ K Q 7
- ♥ Q 10 8
- ♦ K J 3
- ♣ Q J 8 4

Partner	You
1♠	?

5
- ♠ A Q 8 3
- ♥ 4
- ♦ A 5
- ♣ A K J 9 7 4

Partner	You
1♠	?

6
- ♠ K Q J 9 5
- ♥ A 5
- ♦ K Q 4
- ♣ Q 5 3

Partner	You
	1♠
2NT	?

7
- ♠ K J 7 4 2
- ♥ 3
- ♦ A 5 3 2
- ♣ K Q 5

Partner	You
	1♠
2NT	?

8
- ♠ K Q 7 6 3
- ♥ Q 3 2
- ♦ K J 4
- ♣ Q 3

Partner	You
	1♠
2NT	?

9
- ♠ J 9 7 6 3
- ♥ A K 4
- ♦ A 4
- ♣ K J 5

Partner	You
	1♠
2NT	?

10
- ♠ K Q 7 5 3 2
- ♥ —
- ♦ A Q 10 8 4
- ♣ K 4

Partner	You
	1♠
2NT	?

ANSWERS

1   2NT   You have enough points to insist on game as well as four-card spade support. Be aware, however, that having made this bid you are completely minimum.

2   2NT   This time you have lots of extra values, but the best way to start is with 2NT and see whether partner can tell you anything useful. For example, if partner bids 3♦ next (showing a singleton or void in diamonds) then you will be well on your way to bidding a grand slam.

3   2♣   You used to bid 2NT on this type of hand, but you can no longer do so. Bid 2♣ intending to bid 3NT next round.

4   2♣   There is a conventional alternative here, if you and your partner wish to play it. You can use 3NT to show exactly this hand: three-card spade support, values for game, 4-3-3-3 shape, and no real slam interest.

5   3♣   Yes, you have game values and four-card spade support, but that doesn't mean you should always bid 2NT if there is a more descriptive bid available. On the assumption that you play jump shifts as strong, we suggest 3♣ here. If you play weak jump shifts, you should start with 2♣ on this hand. There will be plenty of time to support spades later.

6   3♠   Balanced, extra values, and good trumps. Perfect!

7   3♥   This says nothing about your hand other than telling partner you have at most a singleton heart. You can tell him you are minimum later by failing to co-operate with any slam tries he makes.

8   4♠   You are not really sorry you opened this hand, especially now you've found a spade fit. However, it's not really suitable for slam unless partner has a super hand. Tell him you are minimum and balanced by jumping to game immediately, and leave any further moves to him.

9   3NT   You have extra values, but you are balanced, and it is important that partner knows you have bad trumps. Even though you may have plenty of high card points, you certainly don't want to reach 6♠ if partner's trumps are ♠Q542 or even ♠K542.

10   4♦   Anything from 4♠ to 7♦ or 7♠ are possible contracts, so tell partner you have a good two-suited hand and leave him to judge how well the hands fit together.

CHAPTER 10

SPLINTER BIDS

WHAT'S IN A NAME?

Dorothy Hayden Truscott *is usually credited with having developed the idea of splinter bids in 1964. However, Lt. Col. Beasley, playing for England in the first official World Championship in 1933 against Ely Culbertson's American team, made up a bid much like a modern splinter in the middle of an auction, eventually reaching a good slam on a combined 22 high card points. Culbertson himself had toyed briefly with the idea of 'void-showing' bids, but discarded it.*

In the last chapter we saw how you could bid 2NT in response to partner's major-suit opening to show a good hand with excellent trump support. A splinter bid shows a similar type of hand but gives partner some additional information. It also has the virtue of using a series of bids that are not used for anything else: a double jump in a new suit over a major-suit opening bid.

Partner	You	
1♠	4♣, 4♦, 4♥	(splinter bids)

Partner	You	
1♥	3♠, 4♣, 4♦	(splinter bids)

All these sequences are **splinter bids**. They show a game raise in partner's major, and a singleton or void in the suit into which you splintered. In one go, a splinter bid tells partner all of the following things about your hand:

1) *You have at least four-card support for his major.*
2) *You have 13-15 points (including distribution).*
3) *You have a singleton (or void) in the bid suit.*

Here's a typical hand on which to respond 4♣ when partner opens 1♠:

♠ A 8 7 6 3　♥ K Q 4　♦ Q 9 8 3　♣ 6

Notice that it fits all three of our criteria. Notice, too, that you're not giving up anything by using the double jump for a splinter. Let's say partner opens 1♠. With a decent club suit and enough values to bid at the two-level, you could bid 2♣. With a club suit and a very good hand, you would jump to 3♣. With a weak hand and lots of clubs, you don't want to preempt now partner has opened the bidding — it still may be your hand. Since you do not need a bid of 4♣ to show clubs, that bid is much more useful for something else — a splinter.

Why are splinters so useful?

The splinter bid is considered to be a particularly useful convention because it helps the partnership get to slams with fewer points than normal, based on precise knowledge of distribution. Remember in Chapter 6 when we discussed Blackwood? We told you that you could not ask partner about aces when you had two or more small cards in a suit, since if there was an ace missing you would not know if the opponents could cash the ace and king. This hand illustrates how playing splinters might solve that problem:

Partner	You
♠ K Q 10 9 2	♠ A 8 7 6 3
♥ A	♥ K Q 4
♦ A K 5 2	♦ Q 9 8 5
♣ 9 7 2	♣ 6

If you just bid 4♠ over partner's 1♠ opener (or a 3♠ forcing raise or Jacoby 2NT) he cannot know whether to bid beyond game or not. Blackwood doesn't help since when you show one ace he would still have no idea whether the opponents could cash the first two or three clubs.

Now see how much easier things are after the auction starts 1♠-4♣. Now partner has a very good hand. Your trumps will certainly be able to take care of his second and third club loser and thus he can now safely bid Blackwood. When partner finds that you have an ace, he can jump to slam. Despite there being only 27 HCP between the two hands, twelve tricks are easy.

What do you do over partner's splinter?

With a minimum hand, or a hand with wasted values, you sign off in four of the agreed major. Partner has already bid his hand completely, so passes. With slam interest — extra values and no wastage in the splinter suit — you can bid something else to make a slam try (see Chapter 14 on cuebids, for example). With the right hand (as in the example we just gave), you can use Blackwood.

Can opener ever make a splinter bid?

Certainly — and the same rules apply. If a jump in a new suit would be forcing, then a double jump shows a singleton or void in the bid suit and a good fit for partner, although of course opener needs a much better hand than 13-15 points.

♠ K Q 9 4   ♥ A K 9 8 3   ♦ A Q 4   ♣ 5

You open 1♥ and partner responds 1♠. What a hand you are going to put down as dummy! You could just jump to 4♠, and that would tell partner you have a super hand with good spade support. Wouldn't it be nice to be able to tell him about the singleton club on the way? Think about it... 2♣ now would show a club suit. A jump to 3♣ would be forcing and show a very good hand with hearts and clubs. So you never need a double jump to 4♣ to show a club suit. Therefore, you are free to use it as a splinter on a hand such as the one above. Remember though, that partner need not have more than 6-7 points for his 1♠ bid, so you need at least 18-19 points for this kind of splinter bid as opener.

To see just how useful this information is to partner, consider two similar hands that he may have for his 1♠ response to 1♥. You hold the hand above, and your second call is a splinter bid of 4♣:

Partner	You
♠ A J 8 3 2	♠ K Q 9 4
♥ 6	♥ A K 9 8 3
♦ K 9 8	♦ A Q 4
♣ 9 7 3 2	♣ 5

On this hand, the news that you have four spades and at most one club is enough to get partner very excited. With 18-19 points, you must have some high cards in diamonds to go with his king. As you can see, twelve tricks in spades is comfortable despite a combined holding of 26 HCP.

Partner	You
♠ A J 8 3 2	♠ K Q 9 4
♥ 6	♥ A K 9 8 3
♦ 9 7 3 2	♦ A Q 4
♣ K 9 8	♣ 5

However, if partner has this hand the information that you have short clubs is terrible news. Undoubtedly, the ♣K is wasted, and partner has no help to bolster either of your red suits. He should bid 4♠ quickly and hope things don't break too badly so that you will at least make game.

Can you splinter with a singleton honor?

As a final note, you will have noticed that we have assumed that honors in a suit other than the splinter suit are useful as we can expect partner to have high cards there. By the same token, we downgrade honors in the splinter suit as wasted values when deciding whether to bid on. At the same time, the splinter is a limited bid; if partner 'knows' you have no high cards in your singleton, he can count on their being in the other suits and bid accordingly. For these reasons, you should avoid making a splinter when you have a singleton ace or (even worse) king. Partner will base his bidding on your high cards being outside your short suit.

Summary

✓ A double jump in a new suit in response to partner's major-suit opening shows at least four-card support, 13-15 points, and at most a singleton in the bid suit.

✓ A double jump in a new suit by opener shows an excellent fit for responder's suit, a shortage in the bid suit, and the values for game opposite even a minimum response (18-19 points).

✓ Do not splinter into suits containing a singleton ace or king.

SPLINTERS

NOW TRY THESE...

What is your next bid on each of the following hands?

1 ♠ A J 4
   ♥ K J 9 2
   ♦ 3
   ♣ Q 10 8 5 3

You	Partner
	1♥
?	

2 ♠ 4
   ♥ A Q 9 3 2
   ♦ K 7 3
   ♣ K 9 6 2

You	Partner
	1♥
?	

3 ♠ 4
   ♥ A Q 9 3
   ♦ A J 3
   ♣ K Q J 7 3

You	Partner
	1♥
?	

4 ♠ K Q 9 3
   ♥ A K J 2
   ♦ 8
   ♣ A 8 5 2

You	Partner
	1♥
?	

5 ♠ A 3 2
   ♥ Q 10 8 5 3 2
   ♦ —
   ♣ K 10 9 4

You	Partner
	1♥
?	

6 ♠ K Q 10 5
   ♥ A Q 4
   ♦ A K 9 8 6
   ♣ 4

You	Partner
1♦	1♠
?	

7 ♠ A K 9 4
   ♥ A 9 3
   ♦ Q J 8 6 4
   ♣ 3

You	Partner
1♦	1♠
?	

8 ♠ A J 10
   ♥ K 6 3
   ♦ A K 10 8 7 3
   ♣ 3

You	Partner
1♦	1♠
?	

9 ♠ K 9 4 2
   ♥ A K Q 4
   ♦ A Q J 9 5
   ♣ —

You	Partner
1♦	1♠
?	

10 ♠ A Q 10 4
   ♥ K 4
   ♦ A K Q 10 4
   ♣ 9 2

You	Partner
1♦	1♠
?	

ANSWERS

1 **4♦** This hand is a minimum for a splinter in terms of both points and distribution, but 4♦ is clearly the most descriptive bid you can make.

2 **3♠** You shouldn't be much better than this for a splinter — a 15-count including distribution.

3 **3♣** Assuming that you play strong jump shifts, this is the right way to start describing this hand. If you play weak jump shifts, then start with 2♣. You are too strong for a splinter bid of 3♠, while Jacoby 2NT (if you play it) doesn't let partner in on the news that you have a source of tricks in clubs.

4 **2NT** This time, start with a Jacoby forcing raise. This hand is too strong for a splinter (showing 13-15 points) whereas Jacoby 2NT is unlimited. Besides, if partner shows a singleton club you will be off to the races, but opposite a singleton spade you will tread more warily.

5 **4♦** Although you have only 9 HCP, this hand is plenty good enough for a splinter. You could reach a good slam if partner has as little as ♠K 4 ♥K 9 7 6 4 ♦J 6 3 2 ♣A 2 (11 HCP to go with your 9!).

6 **4♣** Once you add your distributional points to your HCP your hand is quite strong enough to insist on game facing even a minimum response. Rather than just bidding 4♠, let partner know about your club shortness in case that is just the information he needs to bid a slam.

7 **3♠** This is not a weak bid, but you are not quite good enough to bid game facing a 6-7 count.

8 **3♦** Your hand looks strong enough to bid 4♣, but there is no guarantee that partner has more than four spades and thus you cannot afford to bypass 3NT. Don't splinter as opener without at least four-card support.

9 **2♥** Bidding 4♣ does not do justice to this monster — it's too good! Start with 2♥ (a reverse and thus forcing — see Chapter 5). You always intend to play in spades, but there is no rush to get the bidding to the four-level on this hand.

10 **4♠** The jump raise to game carries the information that you have a strong hand with four-card spade support but no shortness.

CHAPTER 11

CUEBID RAISES

WHAT'S IN A NAME?

♥ When you bid a suit that has already been bid naturally by the opponents, you are said to make a **cuebid**. In the early days of bridge, this kind of bid was used to show a singleton or void in the opponents' suit, and a very strong hand. The modern approach is more flexible, and you will encounter cuebids in dozens of different low-level situations.

In future chapters we shall introduce numerous situations in which you can make use of a bid in the opponents' suit. Such bids are called **cuebids**. In this chapter, we're going to talk about two situations where being able to add the cuebid to your arsenal increases the options available to you to raise partner's suit.

LHO	*Partner*	*RHO*	*You*
	1♥	pass	?

Without the overcall, you have the following choices if you want to raise hearts:

2♥	6-9 points, 3+ hearts
3♥	10-12 points, usually 4+ hearts
4♥	distributional, 5+ hearts
other	Jacoby 2NT, splinters, (see Chapters 9 and 10)

LHO	Partner	RHO	You
	1♥	2♣	?

Now let's suppose partner has opened 1♥ and they have overcalled 2♣, and it's your turn to bid. Now that they have bid, things have changed. In the first place, 2NT is no longer Jacoby — it reverts to its natural meaning, a balanced, invitational hand with stoppers in their suit. Secondly, you may want to jam their auction somewhat, with some heart length and not many high cards, especially at favorable vulnerability. Enter the cuebid — the bid of the opponents' suit.

If you use the cuebid of 3♣ here to show a limit raise or better in hearts, you can let 2NT revert to its natural meaning, and also have 3♥ available if you want to preempt. Let's look at how this works in some examples:

♠ K 7 2   ♥ Q 10 2   ♦ J 8 5 4 2   ♣ 8 6

If RHO had passed, then you would have raised to 2♥. The overcall doesn't change that. In a competitive auction, it is even more important to tell partner than you have some values and that you like his suit. Bid 2♥.

♠ 10 7 2   ♥ Q 10 7 3   ♦ K 8 5 4 2   ♣ 8

You could bid 2♥ with this hand too, but wouldn't it be nice to be able to preempt? Perhaps the opponents can get together in spades if you leave them room. At the very least, you would like to stop LHO being able to raise to 3♣. Playing cuebid raises, you can safely jump to 3♥ on this hand and partner will know you are preempting.

♠ 10 7   ♥ K 10 7 3 2   ♦ K 8 5 4 2   ♣ 8

Playing cuebid raises, all direct raises of hearts are preemptive so you can safely bid 4♥ now. Partner won't go looking for a slam.

♠ A 7 2   ♥ Q 10 7 3   ♦ K Q 5 2   ♣ 8 6

What do you do with a 'real' high-card raise of hearts, though? As you have no doubt realized by now, you start with a cuebid of the opponent's suit. This time you have a genuine invitational 3♥ bid — a limit raise. Start with a cuebid — 3♣. All this says to partner is 'I have at least a raise to 3♥.' The cuebid shows a limit raise or better.

What happens after you make a cuebid raise?

Partner should bid over your cuebid as though you have made a limit raise. In other words, with a minimum 1♥ opening, partner will bid 3♥. Now, if you only have a limit raise, you can pass. If you have a little more, you can raise to game. If partner has better than a minimum hand, he should bid game himself directly over the cuebid. If he has a really good hand with slam interest, he can safely proceed beyond game knowing that you have at least a limit raise.

Raising partner's overcall

LHO	Partner	RHO	You
1♦	1♠	pass	?

One of the most important uses for cuebids is to show a good raise of partner's suit when he has overcalled. Again, in a competitive auction, it's very useful to be able to reserve jump raises for preemptive purposes, to get in the opponents' way, and use the cuebid to show a good raise for partner.

♠ K 8 4　♥ J 8 3 2　♦ 5 3　♣ K 10 7 2

First let's point out that when you have support for partner, you should show it as fast as you can. On this hand you don't have much, but do you really want to pass? Partner might have quite a good hand and he would love to hear that you have some support for his spades. Perhaps you think that you can pass for now, and then bid spades later if LHO bids again? That strategy will work if the auction goes

LHO	Partner	RHO	You
1♦	1♠	pass	pass
2♦	pass	pass	?

Now you can bid 2♠ and everyone will be happy. But if it goes

LHO	Partner	RHO	You
1♦	1♠	pass	pass
2♣	pass	3♣	?

Are you now going to bid 3♠? It might be correct to do so, but it might equally be a disaster. If you raise to 2♠ on the first round of the auction, then partner can compete to 3♠ when he has a good hand, but stay out of trouble when he does not.

There is also another significant advantage of bidding on the first round. You will have noticed that LHO has bid clubs now, which his partner likes. Chances are favorable that if you had raised to 2♠, LHO would not have been able to bid 3♣ all on his own. That's right, your pass has made things easy for the opponents to find their fit.

OK, so you are now convinced that you should raise partner's overcall despite having a fairly poor hand. Similarly, with more spades you can make a preemptive jump raise

♠ K 8 4 3 2　♥ J 8 3　♦ 3　♣ K 10 7 2

Don't be afraid to bid 3♠ on this hand, whatever the vulnerability. Now let's give you

♠ K 8 4　♥ A J 8 3　♦ 5 3　♣ K 10 7 2

This time you have what you might term a 'real' raise — you want to invite partner to bid game if he has a good overcall (a limit raise, in fact). Since you would raise to 2♠ or 3♠ with much weaker hands with support, clearly you must find a different bid on this hand. This is the hand on which you can make use of the cuebid of the opponent's suit. So this time bid 2♦. This says to partner, 'I have a good raise of your suit to at least the two-level. Do you have anything extra?' Think of this cuebid as showing a limit raise or better.

LHO	Partner	RHO	You
1♦	1♠	pass	2♦

BY THE WAY

If you play a cuebid to guarantee support for partner after he has overcalled, then you need to be able to do something to show a good hand that doesn't have support for partner. Most players solve this by agreeing that a new suit bid by an unpassed hand is forcing for one round.

With a minimum overcall, partner will simply rebid his suit at the lowest available level. If he does that, you will be happy to pass with the hand above. If you have a little more than this but still not enough to go right to game, you can then raise to 3♠. This would be a very strong invitation that partner should only pass with a terrible overcall.

If partner has a good overcall, he can do lots of things. He can jump to 3♠ over your cuebid to show a little extra or he can go straight to game himself. He can also bid a second suit or even make a slam try.

Summary

✓ When partner opens and RHO overcalls, a cuebid of the opponents' suit shows a limit raise or better.

✓ Partner bids over the cuebid as though you had made a limit raise. If you have more than that, you can decide whether to bid on depending on partner's actions.

✓ If RHO overcalls, all direct raises show less than a limit raise.

✓ A cuebid of the opponent's suit after partner has overcalled shows a limit raise or better. Partner bids as though you had shown a limit raise. If you have more than that, you can decide whether to bid on depending on partner's actions.

✓ All direct raises of partner's overcalled suit are preemptive, showing good trumps but weakish hands.

CUEBID RAISES

NOW TRY THESE...

What is your next bid on each of these hands?

1
- ♠ K 6 3
- ♥ J 7 5 3 2
- ♦ 6 3
- ♣ K 6 3

LHO	Partner	RHO	You
1♦	1♠	pass	?

2
- ♠ A J 7
- ♥ K J 7 4
- ♦ 6 4
- ♣ A 7 4 3

LHO	Partner	RHO	You
1♦	1♠	pass	?

3
- ♠ K Q 8 4
- ♥ A K 6 3
- ♦ 7 5
- ♣ A Q 5

LHO	Partner	RHO	You
1♦	1♠	pass	?

4
- ♠ Q 10 8 4
- ♥ 3
- ♦ 9 5 3
- ♣ A 8 5 4 2

LHO	Partner	RHO	You
	1♠	2♦	?

5
- ♠ A Q 3
- ♥ A K 4
- ♦ 5 4
- ♣ K J 6 4 3

LHO	Partner	RHO	You
	1♠	2♦	?

6
- ♠ A Q 7 4
- ♥ A K J 7 4
- ♦ 5
- ♣ K 6 4

LHO	Partner	RHO	You
	1♠	2♦	?

7
- ♠ A J 8 7 3
- ♥ J 6 4
- ♦ 5
- ♣ K 6 4 2

LHO	Partner	RHO	You
		1♦	1♠
pass	2♦	pass	?

8
- ♠ A K 6 4 2
- ♥ A J 6
- ♦ 7 4
- ♣ K 5 3

LHO	Partner	RHO	You
		1♦	1♠
pass	2♦	pass	?

9
- ♠ K Q 9 6 3
- ♥ 8 5 3
- ♦ A 9 5
- ♣ K 3

LHO	Partner	RHO	You
			1♠
2♣	3♣	pass	?

10
- ♠ K Q J 8 6 4
- ♥ K Q 10 7
- ♦ A K
- ♣ 3

LHO	Partner	RHO	You
			1♠
2♣	3♣	pass	?

ANSWERS

1 **2♠** Raise now, as you may not get another chance.

2 **2♦** Tell partner you have a decent hand with spade support. If partner can only rebid 2♠, then you will pass.

3 **2♦** You know you are going to bid at least 4♠, but bid 2♦ for now and see whether partner is better than minimum.

4 **3♠** You have a bad hand but a nice fit for partner's spades. Bid as much as you dare (perhaps even 4♠ not vulnerable against vulnerable opponents). The objective is to try to stop LHO bidding hearts, where they almost certainly have a good fit.

5 **3♦** Start by telling partner that you have a nice hand with spade support. You are going to raise to game even if partner shows a minimum by rebidding 3♠, and if he does more than that then a slam is quite possible.

6 **2♥** You could bid 3♦ to show spade support, but there is no rush. Start by showing your hearts. 2♥ is forcing, just as it would be if RHO had passed. There will be plenty of time to support spades later. Always try to choose the sequence that provides partner with the maximum amount of information.

7 **2♠** You are not proud of your overcall. Better tell partner that you have a minimum.

8 **4♠** Even if partner has a minimum cuebid (about 11-12 points and three-card support) you want to play in game.

9 **3♠** You have a minimum opening. What bidding 3♠ now says to partner is 'If the auction had gone 1♠-3♠ I would have passed'.

10 **4NT** As partner has enough for a limit raise, you expect to make lots of tricks. Just check how many aces (if any) are missing, then bid 5♠, 6♠ or 7♠.

BALANCING

WHAT'S IN A NAME?

♥ ***Balancing*** *means reopening with a bid or a double after the bidding has stopped at a low level. In the U.K. it is called 'protecting', which is a more descriptive word. The objective many times is to 'protect' your partner, who may have been kept out of the auction by the opponents' bidding.*

When the opponents try to end the auction at a low level, and you have to decide whether to let them, you are said to be in the 'balancing seat'. The most common situation is when LHO opens the bidding and two passes follow.

LHO	*Partner*	*RHO*	*You*
	(direct seat)		*(balancing seat)*
1♥	pass	pass	?

If you decide to take action here, by overcalling or making a takeout double, you are said to be 'balancing'. There is virtually no hand you can have on which you would have made a positive bid in second seat that would pass here. However, as we shall see, you should bid on hands in the balancing seat that you would pass automatically if partner still had a chance to bid. Let's investigate why.

When you are considering whether to balance, you are not only bidding your own hand, but also protecting partner. Why does partner need protecting? Think about his problem with this hand after the 1♥ opening:

BY THE WAY

Balancing is not strictly speaking a convention but really is a question of judging whether or not you should bid, and if so, what you should bid. We have included the topic of balancing in this book as it is an area of bidding that causes less-experienced players a great deal of trouble.

♠ 9 4   ♥ A K 3   ◆ A J 6 5   ♣ J 9 6 2

You will realize that there was little partner could do except pass over 1♥. He is not strong enough for 1NT, he doesn't have a 5-card suit to overcall, and he has the wrong shape (length in the opponents' suit and shortage in the other major) to make a takeout double.

Let's say your hand in the balancing seat is:

♠ J 8 3 2   ♥ 5   ◆ K 10 7 4   ♣ K Q 7 5

If RHO opened 1♥, you would pass because you are not strong enough to make a takeout double. However, if the auction starts with 1♥ on your left and two passes follow, the requirements for a takeout double are much lower. Looking at the two hands above together, it is clear that you do not want to sell out to 1♥. Chances are that the opponents can make seven or eight tricks in hearts while you can probably make nine tricks in clubs or diamonds. One of you obviously has to bid. Since partner cannot reasonably bid in the direct seat, you have to take some action now.

How much less do you need to balance ?

In the balancing seat, you must be more aggressive. A good guide is to add a king (or 3 points) to the value of your hand and then bid whatever you would have if RHO had opened. It may sound incredibly dangerous to bid a hand that you don't actually hold, but there is logic to this principle.

BY THE WAY

It is seldom (and many people would say never) right for you to allow your opponents to play a suit contract at the one-level.

Let's say you have the 9-point hand given above. LHO's 1♥ opening showed 13-19 points and RHO cannot have more than 5 points having passed his partner's opening bid. Thus, the opponents have at most 24 points and perhaps as few as 13. Even if both opponents are maximum, partner will have 7 points and he could have as many as 18 (and certainly as many as 15 in a hand that had no suitable action available over 1♥). The chances are that the points are split about evenly between the two sides. If that is the case, you can surely make a partscore.

In addition, if the opponents have the balance of points then the chances are that they will bid again. Then at least you have pushed them higher and they will have to work that much harder to make their contract. Perhaps they'll go down.

How do you bid after partner balances?

Every silver lining has a cloud wrapped around it! As partner has mentally added a king to his hand, you must deduct one from yours. When deciding how high to bid facing a balancing bid, take a king off your actual point count and then bid what you would have bid had partner been in direct seat.

Notrump bidding offers a straightforward illustration of how this works. These are the normal point ranges for notrump responses to a direct takeout double:

LHO	Partner	RHO	You
1♥	dbl	pass	?

1NT	=	8-10 points
2NT	=	11-12 points
3NT	=	13+ points

But if partner *balances* with a double, you must have a king more in each case:

LHO	Partner	RHO	You
		1♥	pass
pass	dbl	pass	?

1NT	=	11-13 points
2NT	=	14-15 points
3NT	=	not possible

When partner doubles in direct seat (immediately after the opening bidder), you know he will have 13+ points, and so you can bid game with a good 13. When he doubles in the balancing seat, he may only have something like the 9-point hand we saw above. If you were too weak to overcall 1NT immediately, then it is not possible for you to have enough high-card points to bid 3NT now.

When bidding suits, the same principles apply. Take a king (or 3 points) from your hand, then bid as you would have if partner had made a direct-seat takeout double, jumping to the two- or three-level if that is appropriate. There is one other possibility, of course, which is the penalty pass:

♠ A Q 10 9 6 4   ♥ A 5   ♦ K 7 4   ♣ K 2

LHO	Partner	RHO	You
		1♠	pass
pass	dbl	pass	?

Sometimes Christmas comes early. The reason you passed over 1♠ on this hand was that you were going to open 1♠ yourself. This was a trap pass. Partner 'protects' with a double (not a shock that he's short in spades, is it?) and you will happily pass, converting partner's balancing double into a penalty double. You could pick up 1100 or 1400 on a good day.

Balancing bids other than 'double'

Suit overcalls retain their normal meaning, and as usual you should have a decent five-card suit. Again, in the balancing seat, you can be a touch more aggressive in terms of hand strength.

If your hand is flat, and you have the requisite stopper in the opponents' suit, you also have the option of balancing with a 1NT bid. Once again, you can mentally borrow a few points from partner's hand. You should agree on a specific range for a balancing 1NT with your regular partner, but something like 11-14 points would be considered standard. Indeed, if you are a passed hand, you can safely bid 1NT with as little as 10-12 points. Remember, partner knows you have passed and thus you cannot have more than that.

Is this the only balancing situation?

No, there are many. Another common situation in which you should consider making a balancing bid on the assumption that partner has some values that he was unable to show occurs when the opponents find a fit and then stop at a low level. In this case, it is also virtually certain that you have a fit too. For example:

LHO	Partner	RHO	You
		1♥	pass
2♥	pass	pass	?

You know that the opponents have only half (or just over) of the high-card points. Both opponents have limited their hands — LHO by his simple raise, and RHO by his failure to look for game.

There are two possible reasons that partner has not bid. One is that he does not have enough values. The second, and far more likely, particularly if you are fairly short in the opponents' suit, is that he had no suitable bid available. If you have the right shape, feel free to overcall or make a takeout double on fewer values than you would if either opponent were still unlimited. Again, mentally adding a king to your hand is a good way to help make the decision.

Summary

✓ It is rarely right to sell out to a suit contract at the one-level. You should try to push the opponents higher, where they might go down, or find a makable contract yourself.

✓ After an opening bid is followed by two passes, you should add a king (or 3 points) to your actual point-count and then overcall, double or bid 1NT depending on your shape.

✓ When partner makes a balancing bid, remember to deduct a king from your values before responding.

✓ If the opponents stop at a low level having found a fit, feel free to overcall or make a takeout double with the right distribution even with fewer values that you normally need for that action.

B A L A N C I N G

NOW TRY THESE...

What is your next bid on each of these hands?

1
- ♠ 8 6 4
- ♥ A 7
- ♦ K J 9 6
- ♣ A 10 8 4

LHO	Partner	RHO	You
1♦	pass	pass	?

2
- ♠ K 4 2
- ♥ K 8 6 5 2
- ♦ 8
- ♣ J 9 5 2

LHO	Partner	RHO	You
1♦	pass	pass	?

3
- ♠ 10 8 7 3
- ♥ A J 8 3
- ♦ 8 2
- ♣ K Q 8

LHO	Partner	RHO	You
1♦	pass	pass	?

4
- ♠ K Q 8
- ♥ A 8
- ♦ K Q 8 4
- ♣ K 10 7 3

LHO	Partner	RHO	You
1♦	pass	pass	?

5
- ♠ J 3
- ♥ K J 8 3
- ♦ A 7 4
- ♣ Q 9 8 3

LHO	Partner	RHO	You
		1♥	pass
pass	dbl	pass	?

6
- ♠ J 3
- ♥ 8 2
- ♦ K 8 6 2
- ♣ A J 9 7 3

LHO	Partner	RHO	You
		1♥	pass
pass	dbl	pass	?

7
- ♠ J 8 6 3 2
- ♥ A 4 2
- ♦ K Q 4 3
- ♣ 4

LHO	Partner	RHO	You
		1♦	pass
pass	dbl	pass	?

8
- ♠ K 8 3
- ♥ Q 10 7 3
- ♦ Q 8 6 5 3
- ♣ 5

LHO	Partner	RHO	You
		1♦	pass
pass	dbl	pass	?

9
- ♠ K J 5
- ♥ J 6 3
- ♦ A 9 7 2
- ♣ J 7 3

LHO	Partner	RHO	You
		1♥	pass
pass	1♠	pass	?

10
- ♠ 8
- ♥ A J 8 4
- ♦ K Q 8 5 3
- ♣ Q 10 5

LHO	Partner	RHO	You
		1♥	pass
pass	1♠	pass	?

ANSWERS

1 1NT If the 1♦ opening bid were on your right, and you had the ♠K instead of one of the small spades, you would overcall 1NT and consider that a minimum. In balancing seat, bid 1NT with this hand — again, a minimum.

2 1♥ You wouldn't overcall 1♥ with a poor hand and such a weak suit if the 1♦ opening were on your right, but in the balancing seat it is clear to do so. Pretend one of your small clubs is the king, and now you would have a normal direct-seat overcall.

3 dbl Mentally give yourself the ♠K and you can see that you would have a normal takeout double of a 1♦ opening on your right.

4 dbl Why not 1NT, you might think? Even though you have a good hand, you must still mentally add a king for being in the passout seat. Having done so, you have a 20-count! With that much in direct seat you would have to double first, intending to bid notrump next, and you should follow the same plan with this hand in the passout seat. Remember that in balancing seat you can bid 1NT with 12 points, so you cannot make the same bid with 17 HCP; you must differentiate between these hands.

5 1NT You have a good hand, but pretend the ♦A is the jack and it does not look quite as strong. Partner has already overbid by three points, so 1NT is plenty. In other words, as partner is expected to overbid in balancing seat, you must underbid to compensate.

6 2♣ If partner had doubled in direct seat, you would have jumped to 3♣, but opposite a balancing double you need a much better hand to take such action. This one is not close to good enough.

7 2♠ This hand is worth a jump, but only to 2♠. Opposite a direct-seat double you would jump to 3♠, but as you realize by now, you have to underbid by a king in a balancing auction.

8 1♥ If partner had made a direct-seat takeout double you might have considered bidding 1NT. After the balancing double you have a much weaker hand than partner is expecting and 1NT would be a significant overbid (it suggests 11-13 points and you have only 7). Just bid your best suit and hope it all works out. You didn't even think about passing for penalties with this garbage, did you?

9 2♠ With 10 points and a nice fit for partner's suit, you would have been more enthusiastic opposite a direct-seat overcall, but this is facing a balancing bid. You may be too high already.

10 1NT You have a nice hand, but it is not certain that your side has even half of the points and with no fit you should be very wary.

HELP SUIT GAME TRIES

WHAT'S IN A NAME?

♥ **Help suit game tries** *are also sometimes known as 'weak suit game tries'. While there are many other game-try methods available, help suit game tries are by far the most popular and widely used among North American players.*

Partner	You
	1♥
2♥	?

Partner	You
	1♠
2♠	?

What is a 'game try'? When the auction begins 1♥-2♥ or 1♠-2♠, responder's hand is defined within fairly narrow parameters. As opener, it will often be obvious to you to pass because you do not have enough values for game between the two hands. Or you may have a really good hand and will be able to bid game even opposite what is a fairly weak response. However, there are also many hands that fall into the gap between a clear pass and an easy game bid. On those hands you need to consult partner, and to do this you need to make a 'game try'.

Why not just invite by re-raising?

Obviously, after the auction begins 1♠-2♠ you could simply bid 3♠ to ask partner if he has a maximum raise (rather like the familiar 1NT-2NT sequence). That will work some of the time, but involves a significant degree of guesswork by responder. Often, it is not whether he has 9 points rather than 6 that is important, but where those points are located. Consider these two responding hands:

Hand A	♠ Q 8 5	♥ 8 5 3 2	♦ K J 8 5	♣ Q 8
Hand B	♠ Q 8 5	♥ K Q 8 5	♦ 8 5 3 2	♣ J 8

The auction starts

Partner	*You*
1♠	2♠
3♠	

If 3♠ is invitational, do you pass or raise? Presumably, you would raise to game on both hands, since in each case you have a maximum 2♠ bid. Let's give partner a reasonable hand for his bidding:

♠ A K J 9 3 ♥ J 6 4 ♦ 2 ♣ A K 5 4

This is fairly typical of the type of hand on which opener would want to make a game try. Now let's put this hand with each of our two responding hands:

Partner	*Hand A*
♠ A K J 9 3	♠ Q 8 5
♥ J 6 4	♥ 8 5 3 2
♦ 2	♦ K J 8 5
♣ A K 5 4	♣ Q 8

Against 4♠, the opponents can take three heart tricks and ♦A. We have 26 points and a nice spade fit, but 4♠ has no chance. Why? Because the ♦KJ are largely wasted facing opener's singleton.

Partner	*Hand B*
♠ A K J 9 3	♠ Q 8 5
♥ J 6 4	♥ K Q 8 5
♦ 2	♦ 8 5 3 2
♣ A K 5 4	♣ J 8

That's better, isn't it? Now, ten or eleven tricks are likely in spades. Responder has virtually the same hand as before, and yet the difference is enormous. Why? Because the hands fit together nicely — responder's king-queen of hearts are worth two tricks since they are facing opener's weak suit. In fact, responder's hand can be even weaker, and you still would want to be in game as long as the hands fit well:

♠ 10 8 5 3　♥ K Q 8　♦ 8 5 3 2　♣ 8 7

On this hand, you barely scraped up a 2♠ response, but game is better than 50%!

As we have just seen, having your cards in the right place is more important than whether you have 6 points or 9 points for your raise. Help suit game tries are a useful convention to make the decision process easier. To make a help suit game try after the auction 1♠-2♠ or 1♥-2♥, opener simply bids the suit in which he needs help. What should a 'help suit' look like? Anything from three or four small cards to Qxxx — any suit with at least two losers in it would qualify.

So when do you accept the game try?

Remember, you're not being asked whether you have a good hand or a bad hand for your single raise, only whether or not you have the right kind of help. There are two kinds of help that you might be able to offer: the first is high cards in the help suit. Let's look at how this would handle the example hand from before.

♠ A K J 9 3　♥ J 6 4　♦ 2　♣ A K 5 4

Partner	You
1♠	2♠
3♥	

This is a typical 'game-try' auction. On the hand above, partner clearly needs your help to cover his three heart losers. He is not suggesting that hearts should ever be trumps by bidding 3♥ — spades are agreed 100%. He is asking for help in hearts. With this hand

♠ Q 8 5　♥ 8 5 3 2　♦ K J 8 5　♣ Q 8

you should quickly bid 3♠, which says that you have no help in hearts — it is a sign-off that partner must pass. However, with this hand

♠ Q 8 5　♥ K Q 8 5　♦ 8 5 3 2　♣ J 8

you have an excellent heart holding and you should jump to 4♠.

The second kind of help you might have is shortness in the help suit and enough trumps to be able to make some ruffs. Let's keep partner's hand the same but change your hand:

Partner	You
♠ A K J 9 3	♠ Q 8 5 2
♥ J 6 4	♥ 8
♦ 2	♦ 9 7 6 5 2
♣ A K 5 4	♣ Q 9 5

Perhaps you would not even consider raising in the first place with this hand (although you should!), but see what a gold mine you have once opener shows a good hand that needs help in hearts. You are very likely to make eleven tricks. Compare this hand to Hand A above (with much more high card strength, but on which nine tricks was the limit) to see what we mean when we say that it is how the hands fit that is crucial, not necessarily how strong they are.

Notice though, that in the example given, you have four-card trump support. Shortness in partner's 'help-wanted' suit is far less useful if you only have three trumps, since the defense can often limit declarer to one ruff by leading trumps.

Summary

✓ After you raise an opening bid of one of a major to the two-level, a bid of a new suit by opener is a game try asking for help in the suit bid. The game-try suit will be one in which opener has at least two losers.

✓ Facing a help suit game try, you should bid game with a concentration of honors in the help suit.

✓ You should also accept the game try with shortness in the help suit if you have at least four-card trump support.

✓ Without help of either kind, you bid three of the agreed major, which partner must pass.

HELP SUIT GAME TRIES

NOW TRY THESE...

What is your next bid on each of these hands?

1
- ♠ K J 9 6 3
- ♥ A 8
- ♦ A 10 9 4
- ♣ Q 5

Partner	You
	1♠
2♠	?

2
- ♠ A J 9 4 3
- ♥ K 6
- ♦ Q 6 5 4
- ♣ A K

Partner	You
	1♠
2♠	?

3
- ♠ A Q 8 5 3
- ♥ A Q
- ♦ Q 9 5 2
- ♣ A J

Partner	You
	1♠
2♠	?

4
- ♠ A K Q 7 4 2
- ♥ 8
- ♦ K J 2
- ♣ K 5 3

Partner	You
	1♠
2♠	?

5
- ♠ A Q J 5 2
- ♥ A 5 2
- ♦ 6
- ♣ K 9 7 4

Partner	You
	1♠
2♠	?

6
- ♠ K Q J 9 5
- ♥ A J
- ♦ J 7 4 3
- ♣ A 3

Partner	You
	1♠
2♠	?

7
- ♠ K 7 4 2
- ♥ 3
- ♦ Q 6 5 3 2
- ♣ 8 5 3

Partner	You
1♠	2♠
3♥	?

8
- ♠ K 6 3
- ♥ Q 3 2
- ♦ Q J 4
- ♣ J 9 6 3

Partner	You
1♠	2♠
3♠	?

9
- ♠ 7 6 3
- ♥ A K 7 4
- ♦ Q 4
- ♣ 8 7 6 5

Partner	You
1♠	2♠
3♣	?

10
- ♠ K 3 2
- ♥ J 5 3
- ♦ A 8 7 5 2
- ♣ 4 3

Partner	You
1♠	2♠
3♥	?

ANSWERS

1   pass   You do not have a good enough hand to make a game try.

2   3♦   You will not make 4♠ if partner has three small diamonds, but game should be a good bet if he has some help in the suit.

3   4♠   You could bid 3♦ to ask for help in diamonds, but this hand is so good you really should insist on game.

4   4♠   You could ask for help in diamonds or clubs. and if you were a little weaker you would have to guess which to choose. However, with this hand you are just about good enough to bid game and hope partner has some useful bits and pieces.

5   3♣   You could bid 3♥, but you might easily make game even if partner has no help there. The club suit is the place you could really use assistance.

6   3♦   If partner has help in diamonds, you want to play in game. If not, then 3♠ is probably high enough.

7   4♠   A fourth trump and a singleton heart. Even with only 5 HCP this is a very good hand and partner should make at least ten tricks. Hope you don't have too much!

8   pass   Partner is *not* inviting you to raise, despite your maximum. He has made his 3♠ bid purely to make it difficult for the opponents in case they can make something.

9   3♥   We didn't mention this in the chapter, but there is one thing you're allowed to do other than bidding 3♠ or 4♠. Bidding 3♥ here says 'I don't have the club help you want, but I do have a good hand and some goodies in hearts'. Partner may be able to bid a reasonable game now on

       ♠ A K Q 6 3   ♥ Q 6   ♦ K 5   ♣ K 9 3 2

Notice that you can only do this in a new suit below the level of three of the agreed major.

10   3♠   Even though you are maximum for your 2♠ bid, you have no help in hearts.

CHAPTER 14

CONTROL-SHOWING CUEBIDS

WHAT'S IN A NAME?

♥ A **cuebid** is a bid in a suit which cannot possibly be suggesting a trump suit. The use of cuebids to show controls in slam auctions dates back to the early days of contract bridge, and was pioneered by *Lenz, Foster, Reith,* and *Shepard.*

A **control** is exactly what the name implies — it means that you control the suit. Aces and voids are called first-round controls. When you have a first-round control, it means that the opponents cannot lead the suit and take an immediate trick — either you have the ace or you are void and can ruff. You must have first-round control of *at least* three suits in order to make a small slam.

Consider this pair of hands though:

Partner	*You*
♠ A Q 10 7 4	♠ K J 9 5 3
♥ A K 4	♥ Q J 8 3
♦ K Q 7	♦ A J
♣ J 4	♣ Q 7

What more could you want? You have a combined 33 HCP, a solid trump suit, and first-round control in three suits. The vast majority of players who do not

CONTROL-SHOWING CUEBIDS

use cuebids would bid this pair of hands to 6♠. And of course, the opponents can take two tricks right away against a spade slam by leading clubs.

This brings us to second-round controls — singletons or kings. In Chapter 10 we discussed Splinter Bids, which allow you to tell partner you have a singleton (or void) in a specific suit. The reason that information is so useful to partner is that it tells him that you have at most one loser in the suit. Control-showing cuebids are another way of conveying the same information. Learning to use control-showing cuebids will significantly improve your slam bidding — much more so than *any* other method (including any version of Blackwood).

What is a cuebid?

The control-showing cuebid was the single most significant advance in bidding theory ever made, and is far more useful for accurate slam bidding than Blackwood can ever be. Look again at the earlier hand above, as it illustrates one of the reasons why Blackwood is of limited value — it only tells you *how many* aces partner has. Often knowing *which* ace partner has is crucial.

Partner	*You*
♠ A Q 10 7 4	♠ K J 9 5 3
♥ A K 4	♥ Q J 8 3
♦ K Q 7	♦ J 7
♣ J 4	♣ A 7

See the difference here? Responder's hand is two points weaker than before, and yet twelve tricks are now easy. Blackwood will only tell opener that responder has one ace, whereas the crucial information he needs is, 'Which ace?'

Here is another example of a hand on which Blackwood will not help:

♠ A K 8 6 4 2   ♥ —   ♦ K Q 6 3   ♣ K J 8

You	*Partner*
1♠	3♠
4NT	5♦
?	

Now what? Partner has an ace. If he has the ♥A, then the opponents have two aces to take and you will make only eleven tricks. If he has a minor-suit ace, then you want to bid 6♠. The problem, of course, is that you have asked partner how *many* aces he has. What you really need to know is *which* ace (if any) he has.

How do you make a cuebid?

Let's set up some simple rules so that you know when a bid is showing a suit and when it is a cuebid.

1. *A trump suit must have been agreed.*

2. *If you have agreed on a major suit, a new suit above three of your major is a cuebid.*

3. *If you have agreed on a minor suit, then a bid of a new suit above 3NT is a cuebid.*

There is a certain logic to this if you think about it. For example, if partner opens 1♠ and you jump to 3♠, do you think you will ever want to play in a suit other than spades? Therefore, the auction 1♠-3♠-4♣ can conveniently be used to enable opener to show slam interest and a club control. Did you notice that we said that when opener cuebids he automatically shows slam interest? Clearly, in this auction, if he were only interested in game, he would simply raise to 4♠.

Let's look at these rules in a little more detail...

Rule 1. *A trump suit must have been agreed.*

In most cases, a suit must have been bid by one partner and raised by the other for it to be considered 'an agreed suit'. You have to *tell* partner you like his suit *before* you start cuebidding. Unfortunately, as we shall see, there are exceptions to this rule, but auctions such as the following establish an agreed trump suit:

You	Partner
1♠	3♠

Bids of 4♣, 4♦ or 4♥ would now be cuebids.

You	Partner
2♣	2♦
2♥	3♥
?	

Bids of 3♠, 4♣ or 4♦ would now be cuebids.

You	Partner
1♦	1♠
3♠	?

Bids of 4♣, 4♦ and 4♥ would now be cuebids. (Note that 4♦ is a cuebid even though opener previously bid the suit naturally.)

Rule 2. *If your agreed suit is a major, then a bid of a new suit above three of your major is a cuebid.*

You	Partner
1♥	3♥
3♠	

This is a cuebid. After the raise to 3♥, you will never want to play in any suit other than hearts.

You	Partner
1♥	2♥
3♦	

This is *not* a cuebid. Why? Because it is not *above* three of your major. We discussed this auction in Chapter 13 — 3♦ is a help suit game try.

To understand the logic for this rule, remember than you can only cuebid when it is clear you are looking for a slam. If you have agreed a major suit as trumps and bid beyond the three-level in that suit, you are already committed to game; you must therefore be interested in going higher if you do anything other than simply bid game.

Rule 3. *If your agreed suit is a minor, then a bid of a new suit above 3NT is a cuebid.*

You	Partner
1♦	3♦
4♣	

This is a cuebid.

You	Partner
1♦	2♣
3♣	3♥

This is *not* a cuebid as it is below 3NT. At this point, partner is simply showing heart values and inviting you to bid 3NT with a spade stopper. Remember, it must be *clear* that you are looking for a slam for a bid to be a cuebid. In this auction partner might still be investigating the best game.

You	Partner
1♥	2♦
3♦	3♥

Once again, this is *not* a cuebid. Partner is still searching for the right trump suit.

How do you decide which suit to cuebid?

A simple rule when cuebidding is that you begin by showing your *lowest* first-round control. If you bypass a suit (i.e. skip over it) then you specifically *deny* control of that suit. Both members of the partnership continue showing controls 'up the line' — i.e. by making the cheapest available bid of a suit in which they have a control. If you come back on the next round of bidding and cuebid a suit you skipped over earlier, then that shows second-round control. Here's an example to illustrate how this all works:

Partner	You
♠ A K Q 8 4	♠ J 10 7 6
♥ K 8 3	♥ A 7
♦ A Q 8 4	♦ K 7 2
♣ 7	♣ J 8 4 2
1♠	3♠
4♦	4♥
6♠	pass

Let's go through this auction step-by-step. After you jump to 3♠, spades are agreed as trumps. All other bids are cuebids. Partner's 4♦ shows the ace *and denies control of clubs.* You can conveniently join the party now by showing your ace with a 4♥ cuebid. Since he is looking at a singleton club, that is all partner needs to hear, and he can jump to slam.

In this next case, it is not what you bid but what you fail to bid that tells your partner what to do.

Partner	You
♠ A 9 8 6 3	♠ K 7 5 2
♥ K Q 6	♥ J 8 2
♦ K Q 8 3	♦ J 4
♣ A	♣ K Q J 5
1♠	3♠
4♣	4♠
pass	

If you use Blackwood you will at least know that two aces are missing and stay out of slam on these hands, but if trumps do not break 2-2 even 5♠ is too high. Cuebidding keeps you safely at the four-level. The important information is provided by your 4♠ bid. If you had a red-suit ace then you would have cuebid it over partner's 4♣. Partner immediately knows that two aces are missing and he therefore has an easy pass of 4♠.

You will remember that in Chapter 6 we said that you could not bid Blackwood with two losers in an unbid suit. Now we can see how cuebidding solves the problem. This next hand also illustrates why cuebidding is essential to sound slam bidding — or, more specifically, sound non-slam bidding.

Partner	You
♠ A K 10 5 3 2	♠ Q 9 6 4
♥ K 4	♥ A Q J 3
♦ 7 4	♦ 8 3
♣ A K Q	♣ J 6 3
1♠	3♠
4♣	4♥
5♣	5♠
pass	

Note that using Blackwood would not help at all on this hand — partner would discover that all but one ace was present but would still not know whether to bid a slam or to stop at the five-level. Once spades are agreed, partner cuebids 4♣ and you shows your ♥A. When you bid 4♥, you specifically *deny* the ♦A, since you bid your cheapest control first.

However, it is still quite possible that you have ♦K and so partner cannot afford just to sign off in 4♠. When you have run out of first-round controls to bid, *then* you can begin to cuebid second-round controls. Partner cuebids his second-round club control, expecting you to cuebid the ♦K if you have it. Having already denied first-round diamond control, you can safely cuebid 5♦ with only a second-round control. When you bypass diamonds for the second time, partner knows that the defense can cash the first two tricks and gladly passes 5♠.

Summary

✓ Before cuebidding you must explicitly agree on a trump suit.

✓ Cuebidding expressly shows slam interest.

✓ If a major is agreed, bids of new suits above three of the agreed major are cuebids. New suits below this level are game tries.

✓ If a minor is agreed, bids of new suits above 3NT are cuebids.

✓ Cuebid your *lowest* first-round control (ace or void) at each opportunity.

✓ You can *never* cuebid in trumps.

✓ A cuebid in a suit you have already bypassed (i.e. a suit in which you have already denied a first-round control) shows a second-round control (the king or a singleton).

CONTROL-SHOWING CUEBIDS

NOW TRY THESE...

What is your next bid on each of these hands?

1
♠ A J 8 5 3
♥ 5
♦ K J 8 4
♣ A 8 3

Partner	You
	1♠
3♣	?

2
♠ K Q J 6
♥ A Q 9 8 4 2
♦ K 7 4
♣ —

Partner	You
	1♥
3♥	?

3
♠ Q 10 8 5
♥ A 3
♦ K J 9 4
♣ 8 5 3

Partner	You
1♠	3♠
4♣	?

4
♠ 8
♥ A K 8
♦ K J 4
♣ A Q 9 7 5 3

Partner	You
1♦	2♣
3♣	?

5
♠ A K 8 6 4 2
♥ K J 8
♦ K Q 6 3
♣ —

Partner	You
	1♠
3♣	4♣
4♠	?

6
♠ K Q 10 6 4 2
♥ —
♦ K Q J 3
♣ A K 8

Partner	You
	1♠
3♠	4♣
4♥	?

7
♠ A Q 10 9 7 4
♥ A 3
♦ A 6 3
♣ Q 7

Partner	You
	1♠
4♦	?

8
♠ Q J 9 6 3
♥ Q 9 5
♦ K 8
♣ A J 8

Partner	You
	1♠
2♥	3♥
4♦	?

9
♠ Q J 9 6 3
♥ Q 9 5
♦ K 8
♣ A J 8

Partner	You
	1♠
2♥	3♥
4♦	4♥
4♠	?

10
♠ Q 10 5 4
♥ 8 6 4
♦ 7
♣ 9 7 5 3 2

Partner	You
2♣	2♦
2♠	3♠
4♣	4♠
5♣	?

ANSWERS

1 4♠ You are not interested in a slam if all partner can do is invite game, so simply raise to 4♠

2 4♣ Start cuebidding with your lowest first-round control. Do not be tempted to bid 3♠ just because you have a nice suit — that's not what 3♠ tells partner.

3 4♥ Cuebid your first-round control, not your diamond length

4 3♥ Ostensibly, bidding 3♥ shows a stopper for notrump purposes. However, when you later bid more clubs, partner will know that 3♥ was a cuebid.

5 pass Partner has denied holding a red-suit ace. Why risk the five-level when you already know there are two top losers?

6 4NT Blackwood! We have said that you should not use Blackwood when you have a void, but in this case you already *know* that partner has the ace of hearts and does not have the ace of diamonds. If he responds 5♦, you will know the opponents have two aces to take and sign off in 5♠. If he shows two aces, then you can confidently bid 6♠.

7 4♥ Partner has spade support and at most a singleton diamond (see Chapter 10). This suggests that he will have honors in the other three suits, all of which will fit nicely opposite your ♥Ax and ♣Qx.

8 4♥ With such a minimum opening, you cannot proceed beyond the safety of game despite having an ace. Note that you know partner does not have the ♠A, so there is at least one loser there, and the five-level might easily be too high.

9 5♣ Now that partner has continued past game, you can cuebid your club ace. It sounds as though that may be all partner needs to hear to bid a slam.

10 5♦ You don't have a very good hand, but opposite partner's strong bidding you could be much worse. You have already denied first-round diamond control by bidding 4♠, so it's safe to cuebid your singleton now.

CHAPTER 15

GRAND SLAM FORCE

♥The Grand Slam Force was originally known as 'Josephine', and is still sometimes referred to by that name. *Josephine Culbertson (1898-1956)* was the wife of Ely Culbertson, one of the earliest contract bridge experts and bidding theorists, and a tireless promoter of the game. Ely devised the convention and named it after his wife, who wrote about it and publicized it. Today, Josephine Culbertson is generally regarded as having been the stronger player of the two.

Just to confuse you, the **Grand Slam Force** (or GSF as we shall call it hereafter) is something of a misnomer since it is not forcing to a grand slam. It starts with a bid of 5NT (which you will admit has very few natural applications) in certain auctions. It is a bid you will use only rarely, however, since it asks partner one very simple question: 'Do you have two of the top three trump honors?' Its value is likewise very simple — it is designed to allow you to check on the solidity of your trump suit before bidding a grand slam.

Obviously, you can only use GSF if that specific information is the only thing you need to know in order to bid a grand slam. Since the bid asks specifically about trump quality, you must have an agreed trump suit. You must also know that you have all of the outside suits controlled and the expectation that you can take thirteen tricks provided the trumps are solid.

It is a very simple convention to use. A bid of 5NT, whether or not that bid is a jump, asks partner if he has two top of the top three trump honors. A typical auction might be:

Partner	You
	2♣
2♦	2♠
3♠	5NT

♠ A J 9 8 6   ♥ A K   ♦ A K Q J 4   ♣ A

Here's a hand on which the only thing you are worried about, once partner supports spades, is where the king and queen of spades are. If partner has them, 7♠ must be essentially laydown. The jump to 5NT asks about the top trump honors, and will give you the information you need.

What are the responses to GSF?

Again, the responses are easy to remember. If you have two of the top three trumps (AQ, AK, or KQ), you jump to a grand slam in the agreed suit. With fewer than two top honors, you bid only six of your suit.

Responses to 5NT GSF

With 2 of the top 3 trump honors	Bid seven of your agreed suit
With any other holding	Bid six of your agreed suit

Is 5NT always GSF?

No, it isn't — there are two exceptions (of course!).

1) **You cannot use GSF once you have used Blackwood to ask for aces.**

Remember that when you bid 4NT Blackwood, if you next bid 5NT over partner's reply then you are asking partner how many kings he has. Even if you use a more advanced version of Blackwood (such as Roman Key Card, which can be found in Chapter 20 of this book), you will find that the 5NT bid is always reserved as a continuing part of the Blackwood sequence, and is never GSF. So you cannot use GSF and Blackwood in the same auction.

2) Sometimes 5NT is a quantitative notrump bid.

You should be familiar with the following auctions:

Partner	You
1NT	5NT

Partner	You
2NT	5NT

In each case, your 5NT bid asks partner to bid 7NT with a maximum, and sign off in 6NT with a minimum.

Can you use GSF when no suit has been agreed?

Yes, you can. A jump to 5NT, when no suit has been specifically agreed, agrees partner's last-bid suit. A common situation in which the GSF bid actually agrees partner's suit is after a preempt. For example:

Partner	You
3♥	5NT

or

Partner	You
4♠	5NT

In each case, 5NT agrees partner's suit and asks about his trumps. Of course, you need quite a hand to use the bid — something like

♠ AK87643   ♥ Q5   ♦ AKQJ   ♣ —

would fit the first example auction.

Summary

✓ When a trump suit has been agreed, a bid of 5NT asks partner to bid a grand slam with two of the top three trump honors.

✓ If partner bids 5NT, you are required to jump to seven of your agreed suit with any two of the top three trump honors; with anything less, bid six of your agreed suit.

✓ If no suit has been agreed, the 5NT bid agrees partner's last-bid suit.

✓ You cannot use GSF after using Blackwood, since 5NT in those auctions asks for kings.

✓ You cannot use GSF directly over partner's notrump opening bid or rebid. 5NT in those auctions is quantitative.

GRAND SLAM FORCE

NOW TRY THESE...

What is your next bid on each of these hands?

1
- ♠ Q 7 4 3
- ♥ —
- ♦ A K J 8 6 4
- ♣ A 6 3

Partner	You
1♠	2♦
3♣	?

2
- ♠ —
- ♥ A J 6 5 2
- ♦ K Q 9 6 3
- ♣ A K Q

Partner	You
1♠	2♥
3♥	4♣
4♦	?

3
- ♠ K J 9 7 3
- ♥ K Q 10 8 3
- ♦ A
- ♣ A K

Partner	You
	1♠
3♠	4NT
5♥	?

4
- ♠ A K Q 10 7 3
- ♥ A K 4
- ♦ K 4
- ♣ A 8

Partner	You
3♦	?

5
- ♠ K J 10 8 6 5 3
- ♥ A K 7
- ♦ 5
- ♣ K 4

Partner	You
	1♠
2♣	3♠
5NT	?

6
- ♠ 5 3
- ♥ Q J 8 7
- ♦ K Q 10 9 5
- ♣ K 4

Partner	You
1♠	2♦
5NT	?

ANSWERS

1   5NT   It is just about possible for partner to have a 3♠ rebid without both the ace and king of spades, so bid 5NT just to make sure. You rate to have about sixteen tricks to cash on this hand.

2   5NT   Once partner shows the ♦A by cuebidding (4♦ — see Chapter 14) all you need to know before bidding the grand slam is that the trumps are solid. Bid 5NT and partner will bid 7♥ if he has both the king and the queen of hearts.

3   7♠   Great, partner has both missing aces. All you need to do now is to check that he has the ♠Q. Ah... but you cannot bid GSF after you use Blackwood, since 5NT now would ask for kings, which doesn't help you; you'll just have to shoot 7♠ and hope for the best. See Chapter 20 on Roman Key Card Blackwood for a more sophisticated version of Blackwood which solves this problem.

4   5NT   The jump to 5NT agrees partner's diamonds. If he has ♦AQxxxxx you want to play in a grand slam.

5   6♠   Partner will be disappointed but that's better than playing in 7♠ missing the ace of trumps!

6   7♦   Partner's jump to 5NT agreed diamonds. You don't need to worry about anything else — just answer the question about your top trumps. Partner must have some kind of freak like

♠ A K 10 7 4 2   ♥ A   ♦ A 9 8 6 4 2   ♣ —

C H A P T E R 16

MICHAELS CUEBIDS and UNUSUAL NOTRUMP

Both these conventions allow you to make an overcall that shows two suits at the same time! Neat idea? Let's look at how **Michaels** works:

LHO	Partner	RHO	You
		1♥	2♥

This immediate cuebid of the suit opened by the opposition used to mean that you had a rock-crusher — an opening strong two-bid of your own. However, this doesn't come up too often, so you are not giving up very much by using it for something else. Michaels' idea was to use it to show various two-suited hands. Playing this convention, when the opponent on your right opens a minor, your cuebid tells partner than you have both majors. If the opening bid is in a major, the cuebid shows the unbid major and one of the minors.

Michaels Cuebids

RHO opens

1♣	2♣ shows spades and hearts
1♦	2♦ shows spades and hearts
1♥	2♥ shows spades and a minor
1♠	2♠ shows hearts and a minor

This can really simplify partner's life. It also makes hands that are otherwise difficult to describe much easier to bid. Since bidding offers a very limited vocabulary, any time you can use a bid to tell partner a great deal about your hand all in one go it must be a good thing. Let's say you have the following hand:

♠ A J 8 5 3   ♥ K J 10 7 2   ♦ 3 2   ♣ 6

Your RHO opens 1♣. If you have no way to show both suits, you would presumably overcall 1♠ hoping to get to bid hearts later on. That's all well and good except when the auction proceeds 1NT on your left, 'pass' from partner and 3NT from opener. Clearly this is the opponents' hand and bidding 4♥ will lead to a large penalty, so you have to pass. Perhaps partner has something like

♠ 10 6   ♥ Q 9 8 4   ♦ Q 10 6   ♣ J 9 5 2

Of course, he leads your suit — spades. The effect of this is to establish declarer's ninth trick in spades whereas 3NT would have no chance on a heart lead. Clearly, if you had overcalled 2♣ over RHO's 1♣, showing at least 5-5 in the majors, partner would have had an easy heart lead against 3NT and you would comfortably defeat the opponents' game.

Of course, the information that you have two suits is not only useful when defending. It will sometimes enable partner to bid a low-point-count game that makes because he has a fit with both of your suits. It may also enable him to find a profitable sacrifice. On the hand we just looked at, partner needs very little more to make a heart partscore quite playable, yet you may never have a chance to bid the suit. The playing strength of two-suited hands is well known to all bridge players and with two suits it is much easier to find a fit in partner's hand.

So, what do you have to give up in order to add Michaels to your system? Yes, traditional, old-fashioned, strong, game-forcing cuebids will no longer be possible, but they occur so rarely that it is no hardship to live without them. If ever you should be dealt such a hand, you can just as easily start by making a takeout double (as we discussed in Chapter 2).

What do you need to use Michaels?

Let's start with the shape requirements for a Michaels Cuebid. *You must be at least 5-5 in your two suits.* Never use Michaels with 5-4 shape as partner will bid his hand expecting two five-card suits and will be very disappointed to find that he has misjudged because you are one short. Using Michaels with a 5-4 shape is a surefire way to lose 1100 when all the opponents can make is a game. For the same reason (i.e. partner is likely to misjudge), don't persuade yourself that it's all right to use Michaels with a 6-4 shape just because you have ten cards in your two suits. It's not. *You must have at least five cards in each of your two suits.*

The most common method is to play that the Michaels bidder must have either a weak hand (less than 10 points) or a very strong hand (16+ points). This is known as 'Mini-Maxi Michaels'. If you have a hand in the 10-15 point range (i.e. too good for a weak Michaels bid, but not powerful enough for a strong Michaels) then overcall the higher-ranking suit. With luck, you will get the chance to bid your second suit later. How weak is 'weak', you may ask? Well, not vulnerable against vulnerable opponents after a 1♣ opening on your right, you can bid 2♣ on as little as:

♠ Q 10 8 5 4   ♥ K J 4 3 2   ♦ 6 3   ♣ 7

We cannot promise you will never get hurt, but it is highly unlikely.

The Mini-Maxi agreement is very useful, since without it the cuebid has too wide a range of possible hands. Often, partner will not know whether or not to keep bidding.

How do you respond to Michaels?

With a fit for one of partner's known suits, simply raise to the appropriate level. Bid assuming that partner has a weak hand — he'll carry on if he actually has a Maxi. It is easy to see that after a minor is opened by your opponents, both suits are known when Michaels is used. What about over a major — e.g. 1♥-2♥? Now you know partner has spades, but don't know whether his second suit is clubs or diamonds. That's fine if you have a spade fit, but what about this hand:

♠ 5 2   ♥ Q 10 7   ♦ 7 5 4 3   ♣ 8 6 3 2

LHO	Partner	RHO	You
1♥	2♥	pass	?

You don't much care for partner's spades, but you do know that you have at least a 9-card fit in one of the minors. To find out which one, you bid 2NT now; this is artificial, and tells partner you are not thrilled with spades and would prefer to play in his minor suit (which he will now reveal).

So what is Unusual Notrump?

What if you have the wrong two suits for Michaels? Suppose RHO opens 1♥ and your hand is:

♠ A 7   ♥ 5   ♦ K Q J 8 3   ♣ A Q J 9 2

You cannot make a Michaels cuebid since that would show spades and a minor. Enter the **Unusual Notrump** (or UNT for short) — a jump overcall of 2NT. If you have a very strong balanced hand, you can double first and then bid notrump at your second turn, so you do not need a natural 2NT overcall. UNT is just like Michaels in that it shows two suits and either a weak or a strong hand, but *UNT shows the two lowest unbid suits.* Obviously, if RHO has opened a major, the two lowest unbid suits will always be the minors. If a minor has been opened, then 2NT shows hearts and the other minor (i.e. still the two lowest unbid suits).

The requirements for making a UNT overcall are the same as Michaels. You must be at least 5-5, and the Mini-Maxi agreement is useful. Both your suits are known, and partner simply gives preference at the appropriate level for his hand strength, assuming that you have a weak hand until further notice.

Summary

When an opponent opens the bidding, a direct cuebid of the opponent's suit or an overcall of 2NT both show different two-suited hands.

✓ Cuebidding a minor shows both majors.

✓ Cuebidding a major shows the other major and an unknown minor.

✓ Overcalling 2NT over a major shows both minors.

✓ Overcalling 2NT over a minor shows hearts and the other minor.

✓ You must have at least five cards in each of your two suits.

✓ Both Michaels and UNT show either a weak hand (exactly how weak will depend on the vulnerability) or a very strong hand.

✓ If the Michaels bidder has an unknown suit then his partner can bid 2NT to ask him to bid his second suit.

MICHAELS AND UNUSUAL NOTRUMP

NOW TRY THESE...

What is your next bid on each of these hands?

1
- ♠ A Q J 8 2
- ♥ K Q 10 8 3
- ♦ A 5
- ♣ 4

LHO	Partner	RHO	You
		1♦	*2?D*

2
- ♠ A Q J 8 2
- ♥ 4
- ♦ A 4
- ♣ K Q 10 8 3

LHO	Partner	RHO	You
		1♥	? *2H*

3
- ♠ 5
- ♥ 3
- ♦ Q 10 8 7 5 3
- ♣ K Q J 8 3

LHO	Partner	RHO	You
		1♥	? *9NT*

4
- ♠ A J 10 8 2
- ♥ 4
- ♦ A 4
- ♣ K Q 10 8 3

LHO	Partner	RHO	You
		1♦	? *1S*

5
- ♠ K Q 8 5
- ♥ J 3
- ♦ A 4 3
- ♣ 8 7 6 3

LHO	Partner	RHO	You
1♦	2♦	pass	? *3S*

6
- ♠ K 8 5 4 2
- ♥ K J 3
- ♦ 9 7 4 3
- ♣ 8

LHO	Partner	RHO	You
1♦	2♦	pass	? *2S 4S*

7
- ♠ 6
- ♥ J 8 5 3
- ♦ 9 7 5 3 2
- ♣ Q 8 3

LHO	Partner	RHO	You
1♥	2♥	pass	? *2NT*

8
- ♠ K J 8
- ♥ A Q 7
- ♦ A 4
- ♣ 9 7 5 3 2

LHO	Partner	RHO	You
1♦	2♦	3♦	? *DBL 4D*

9
- ♠ K 2
- ♥ K Q
- ♦ K Q 10 5
- ♣ A J 10 8 3

LHO	Partner	RHO	You
1♦	2♦	pass	? *3NT*

10
- ♠ 3
- ♥ 4 2
- ♦ K J 8 5 3 2
- ♣ 10 6 4 2

LHO	Partner	RHO	You
1♦	2♦	pass	? *2H*

ANSWERS

1   2♦   This shows both majors. As you have the very strong hand type, you intend to bid again even if partner only gives you a simple major-suit preference.

2   2♥   Ideal. A very good hand with five spades and a five-card minor.

3   2NT   Whether you bid on this hand will depend on the vulnerability. Despite only having 8 HCP, your excellent shape gives you good playing strength if partner can fit either or both of your suits. We recommend that you bid 2NT with this hand, but if you're vulnerable against not, discretion should probably persuade you to pass.

4   1♠   You don't have both majors and you don't have the two lowest unbid suits, so you cannot show this two-suited hand with one bid. Overcall 1♠ for now. Perhaps you will have a chance to bid your clubs later.

5   3♠   If partner has a strong hand you expect to make game. If he is weak, then perhaps the opponents can make game. Either way, a jump will get across the message that you have a good fit for one of partner's suits and some values.

6   4♠   Because of the fit for both of partner's suits, you expect to make this contract if he is strong. If he is weak then you know the opponents can make game and this will be a profitable sacrifice. By bidding confidently you hope the opponents will allow you to steal the hand in 4♠ even when partner is weak.

7   2NT   You don't like spades at all, and expect partner's second suit to be clubs. It cannot hurt to bid 2NT to find out, though. On a good day partner will bid diamonds next.

8   4♦   We saw in Chapter 15 that a bid of the opponents' suit at a high level can be used to show a control and suggest slam interest. This cuebid, however, simply asks partner to tell you which major he prefers and shows enough values for game. Neat, huh?

9   3NT   This may not make if partner is very weak, but if you are going to make game it's likely to be in notrump. If you don't bid notrump, no one else will, and if partner is 6-6 in the majors, he'll bid again.

10 2♥   You don't like either of partner's suits and you expect to go minus. The objective is to escape undoubled on what is clearly a misfit. Bid a confident 2♥ and hope partner doesn't raise. One thing is certain, and that is that passing now will give LHO an easy double as he is already known to have diamonds.

CHAPTER 17

LANDY 2♣ over OPPONENTS' 1NT

WHAT'S IN A NAME?

♥ This convention was devised by ***Alvin Landy*** *(1905-1967)* of Cleveland, Ohio. Life Master #24, Landy was one of the founders of the World Bridge Federation. As a player, he won five North American Championship titles.

In the early days of bridge, it was considered very dangerous to enter the auction once the opponents had opened 1NT. After all, usually they have most of the high cards (one hand has at least 15), and you might well be setting yourself up for a large penalty. Modern thinking is exactly the opposite: make life as difficult as you can for your opponents, especially if you have distribution and good playing strength. Today, too, where you may well find your opponents playing a 12-14 notrump opening, or even 10-12, it's important not to get shut out when the hand might actually be yours anyway!

Consider this hand:

Partner	You
♠ A J 8 5 3	♠ 6
♥ K J 9 4	♥ Q 10 8 6 2
♦ K 10 4	♦ A 9 5 2
♣ J	♣ 9 6 4

Partner	You
1♠	1NT
2♥	4♥
pass	

That wasn't too hard, was it? And if nothing bizarre happened, you would be fairly confident about making 4♥. Now see what happens if the opponents get in your way with just one simple bid...

LHO	Partner	RHO	You
1NT	2♠	all pass	

What a difference! Not only have you missed your fairly easy game in hearts, but you have finished in a partscore that is almost certain to fail. Neither of you has even mentioned your side's best suit, hearts.

Of course, you will often arrive in the best contract if you just make a natural overcall of the opposition's 1NT opening. There are two situations, though, where it is difficult to do so. One occurs when you have a two-suited hand, as you have to guess which suit to bid. The other is on hands such as the one above, where the best fit is in the strong hand's secondary suit and his partner does not have a good enough hand to bid.

To address this kind of problem, players have developed numerous conventional methods for defending against 1NT openings. Some are quite complicated and enable you to show all sorts of one- and two-suited hands. The one we are going to describe here only solves your problem when you hold both major suits, but it has the enormous benefit of being the simplest too.

What is Landy?

Landy is one of the easiest conventions to learn and master, and yet one of the most useful too. How does Landy work? Very simply — a bid of 2♣ over an opponent's 1NT opening tells partner that you have both majors.

LHO	Partner	RHO	You
		1NT	2♣

You must have enough values to justify bidding at the two-level, and the vulnerability will be a factor in determining if a marginal hand is strong enough. There is, however, a maximum for the bid — you will not have enough high-card points (about 16+) to double the 1NT bid.

You must also have a hand that is at least 5-4 in the majors. If you are 5-5 or better, then you need fewer high-card points to bid than if you are only 5-4.

What do you do when partner uses Landy?

There are many responding schemes played today, but the following is the one recommended by Alvin Landy himself.

With no interest in game

You will usually just bid your better major suit. However, with a six-card or longer minor and a weak hand you can bid 2♦ or even pass 2♣. Remember, partner cannot have more than 15 HCP, so there is no danger of missing game if you are weak.

If you have enough values to invite game (10-12 points)

You have several choices. If you have a fit for one of partner's suits, you can invite by jumping to 3♥ or 3♠. With no fit, you can bid 2NT or jump to 3♦ (showing a good diamond suit).

If you want to insist on game

You can simply jump to 3NT, 4♥ or 4♠ provided you are sure of which game you should play. If you're not sure where you want to play yet, there is also one artificial bid available — 3♣. This shows a good hand unrelated to clubs. It is forcing and asks partner to bid his longer major. This is a useful tool when you have a good hand with three cards in one major (or in both) as partner will respond by telling you which is his longer suit — remember, he must have at least one five-card major to overcall 2♣.

BY THE WAY

If LHO opens 1NT, and the next two players pass, is 2♣ still Landy? You need to discuss with your partner whether the bid of 2♣ in this auction is still Landy, as it would be directly over the 1NT bid, or whether it shows clubs. Our recommendation is that you do still play it as Landy, but it's entirely up to you.

Partner	You
♠ 7 6	♠ K J 9 5 2
♥ K Q 7	♥ A 10 8 6
♦ K J 10 6 3	♦ Q 2
♣ Q J 6	♣ K 3

LHO	Partner	RHO	You
		1NT	2♣[1]
pass	3♣[2]	pass	3♠[3]
pass	3NT[4]	all pass	

1. Landy.
2. Which is your longer major?
3. Spades.
4. Never mind, then; we'll play here.

Summary

✓ A bid of 2♣ directly over the opponent's 1NT opening shows a hand with at least 5-4 in the majors but not strong enough to double (less than 16 points)

✓ You and your partner can agree to use 2♣ as Landy in the balancing seat over a 1NT opening bid also. We also recommend that you do.

After partner uses Landy 2♣

✓ if you are weak, bid your longer major. You may also pass (with long clubs) or bid 2♦ (with at least a six-card suit).

✓ 2NT and 3♦ are natural and invitational.

✓ jumps to 3♥ and 3♠ invite partner to game in that suit.

✓ 3♣ is an artificial bid and asks partner to describe his hand further, by bidding his longer major.

LANDY 2♣ OVERCALL OF A 1NT OPENING

NOW TRY THESE...

Playing Landy, what is your next bid on each of these auctions?

1
- ♠ K Q 8 4
- ♥ A J 7 4 2
- ♦ A 7 3
- ♣ 4

LHO	Partner	RHO	You
		1NT	?

2
- ♠ K J 6 4 2
- ♥ Q J 10 6 3
- ♦ K 4
- ♣ 7

LHO	Partner	RHO	You
		1NT	?

3
- ♠ A K Q 3
- ♥ Q J 10 8 4
- ♦ A J 4
- ♣ 4

LHO	Partner	RHO	You
		1NT	?

4
- ♠ K Q J 7 4 2
- ♥ Q 9 6 3
- ♦ K 5
- ♣ 4

LHO	Partner	RHO	You
		1NT	?

5
- ♠ K J 5 3
- ♥ A Q 5 2
- ♦ K 6 3
- ♣ J 5

LHO	Partner	RHO	You
		1NT	?

6
- ♠ 8 6 4 2
- ♥ 3
- ♦ J 4
- ♣ J 9 8 6 4 2

LHO	Partner	RHO	You
1NT	2♣	pass	?

7
- ♠ K J 8 4
- ♥ J 4
- ♦ 9 7 4 3
- ♣ A 8 4

LHO	Partner	RHO	You
1NT	2♣	pass	?

8
- ♠ A Q 6
- ♥ K 7 3
- ♦ A Q 8 5 3
- ♣ 9 4

LHO	Partner	RHO	You
1NT	2♣	pass	?

9
- ♠ J 9 7 4 2
- ♥ K 5 4
- ♦ 9 7 5 4 3
- ♣ —

LHO	Partner	RHO	You
1NT	2♣	pass	?

10
- ♠ K
- ♥ Q 5
- ♦ A J 5 3
- ♣ K Q J 9 5 3

LHO	Partner	RHO	You
1NT	2♣	pass	?

ANSWERS

1   2♣   Perfect. Almost enough to double 1NT, but not quite, and 5-4 in the majors.

2   2♣   This is a perfect hand for Landy, because you have 5-5 in the two suits you are showing. Even vulnerable against non-vulnerable opponents, you should overcall with this hand and accept if partner invites game.

3   dbl   You are too strong just to overcall. If you bid 2♣ and partner gives preference to a major at the two-level, you will be tempted to raise because you have extra values. If partner is broke this will be a disaster, while you can beat 1NT with very little assistance from partner.

4   2♠   Not 2♣ this time. Even though you have both majors, it will seldom be better to play in hearts when your spades are so much stronger.

5   pass   You are only 4-4 in the majors. While it is tempting to bid, do not mislead partner.

6   2♠   Partner will have at least four spades, and often five. Do not be tempted to pass just because you are so weak. Remember that partner may have no clubs at all.

7   3♠   Jumping all the way to game will get you too high if partner has tried to compete for the partscore on a minimum hand. Invite with 3♠ and let partner out if he has stretched to overcall in the first place.

8   3♣   This time you can insist on game, but which one? Bidding 3♣ asks partner to tell you which is his better major. When you find out, you can raise to game.

9   4♠   On a good day, this may even make! The opponents have enough values to make at least a partscore and may even be cold for game. Make life hard for the opponents by preempting with such a good fit.

10   3NT   You have a good hand, but it isn't going to fit well so don't be surprised if this doesn't make. You will probably need the clubs to run, and that's something you won't find out about until you see dummy.

SOPHISTICATED STUFF

LEBENSOHL

WHAT'S IN A NAME?

♥ The concept behind the Lebensohl convention was first outlined in *The Bridge World* magazine by **George Boehm** *(1922-1993)*, a prominent player and writer from New York. Boehm attributed the idea to **Ken Lebensold** of Oakland, California, and although Lebensold denied any responsibility for it, his name had already become synonymous with the method. Lebensohl it remains — including the change in spelling!

LHO	Partner	RHO	You	
	1NT	2 of a suit	2NT	*(Lebensohl)*
pass	3♣			

When partner opens 1NT and your RHO overcalls a suit, any suit, all your carefully prepared system goes out of the window. You are past 2♣, so Stayman is no longer available; you can no longer play transfers, and you need to distinguish among a whole range of different hand types and hand strengths. Lebensohl is a convention designed to help you handle this problem.

When you play **Lebensohl**, a bid of 2NT in these sequences is a *relay*, which forces partner to bid 3♣, *whatever his hand*. Note that neither of you is saying anything about clubs — what you have done is to create a situation where the notrump bidder's partner can show a number of different hand types.

BY THE WAY

Lebensohl is an extremely complex convention, and whole books can and have been written about it. You will come across players who have all kinds of different ways of playing Lebensohl. The structure we are describing here is relatively simple, and therefore easy to remember. But, as you become more familiar with it, you and your partner may wish to modify your agreements.

How does it work?

Let's first look at balanced hands, the kind where you would simply have bid 3NT if they hadn't overcalled (for the sake of example, we'll assume they bid 2♠). Now you have two ways to get to 3NT — you can just bid it:

LHO	Partner	RHO	You
	1NT	2♠	3NT

or you can go through Lebensohl first:

LHO	Partner	RHO	You
	1NT	2♠	2NT
pass	3♣	pass	3NT

Remember this phrase: **SLOW SHOWS** (shows a stopper). In the first example, you have the values to raise to 3NT, but *no* spade stopper. Partner passes if he can handle spades, or bids his best suit if he can't. In the second, slow sequence, where you have gone through the Lebensohl relay, you are telling partner not to worry about spades, since you have a stopper yourself: **SLOW SHOWS.**

Can you still use Stayman?

You certainly can, and again there are two possible sequences you can use. A cuebid of the opponents' suit is treated as a Stayman enquiry, and you show or deny a stopper in the overcalled suit depending on whether or not you go through Lebensohl. Again, **SLOW SHOWS.**

BY THE WAY

You will notice that if the overcall is 2♣, you cannot relay and then cuebid (partner will already have bid 3♣!). In this one case, you cuebid immediately as Stayman whether or not you have a club stopper. This problem seldom arises in real life, though, as most opponents will be using 2♣ as some kind of conventional overcall that has nothing to do with clubs.

LHO	Partner	RHO	You
	1NT	2♠	2NT
pass	3♣	pass	3♠

This sequence enquires about hearts, and promises a spade stopper. Partner bids 4♥ if he has four hearts, or 3NT if he does not. On the other hand:

LHO	Partner	RHO	You
	1NT	2♠	3♠

3♠ here is still Stayman, but denies a spade stopper. Now partner (without a heart fit) can bid 3NT only if he can handle spades; failing that, he bids his best suit and you'll have to scramble to find the right place to play the hand.

What about unbalanced hands?

Hands that aren't necessarily headed for 3NT or four of a major are a little trickier. Again, you have two ways to go: you can bid your suit directly, or you can go through Lebensohl first. In all cases, beginning with a Lebensohl 2NT relay shows a weaker hand than does bidding your suit directly at the three-level. Let's see how this allows you to bid hands that want to compete, invite, or force.

> **BY THE WAY**
>
> *Of course, you no longer have a natural invitational 2NT bid available if you use Lebensohl. When you hold that kind of hand, you will have to decide whether to double them for penalties, pass, or pray and bid 3NT. You won't always be right, of course, but it's a small price to pay for what you gain with Lebensohl.*

1. You have a major-suit hand.

♠ 9 7 ♥ A J 9 8 4 ♦ K J 7 ♣ K 7 3

LHO	Partner	RHO	You
	1NT	2♠	3♥

This 3♥ bid is natural and forcing to game. You need 10+ HCP and at least a five-card heart suit. Partner chooses between 4♥ and 3NT. Of course, if he does not like hearts, he needs a spade stopper to bid 3NT; with neither a heart fit nor a spade stopper, he should cuebid 3♠, to ask whether you have a stopper.

♠ 9 7 ♥ Q J 9 8 6 4 ♦ 9 6 3 ♣ Q 6

LHO	Partner	RHO	You
	1NT	2♠	2NT
pass	3♣	pass	3♥

Bidding 3♥ via a 2NT relay says that you only wish to play in a partscore.

In some cases, because of the extra space available, you can make invitational bids in a major. If you have room to bid your suit at the two-level, then you can do so on the competitive hand. Now you can go through Lebensohl with an invitational hand, and jump to three of your suit to create a force:

♠ 9 7 ♥ Q J 9 8 6 4 ♦ 9 6 3 ♣ Q 6

LHO	Partner	RHO	You
	1NT	2♦	2♥

Here you have room to bid 2♥. This is the other case:

♠ 9 7 ♥ A J 9 8 6 4 ♦ 9 6 3 ♣ Q 6

LHO	Partner	RHO	You
	1NT	2♦	2NT
pass	3♣	pass	3♥

Because you could simply have bid 2♥ with a weaker hand (or 3♥ with a stronger one), going through Lebensohl has created an invitational sequence. Partner will pass with a minimum and raise you to 4♥ with a maximum.

2. You have a minor suit.

Usually, when you have a long minor your objective is to get to 3NT. We there-fore recommend that you play direct minor-suit bids as invitational:

♠ 9 7   ♥ Q 5 4   ♦ K Q 10 9 8 6   ♣ 6 4

LHO	Partner	RHO	You
	1NT	2♠	3♦

Partner can bid on with a suitable hand (he could bid 3NT with a spade stopper and a diamond fit, for example) but will pass otherwise. You can use the Lebensohl sequence when you simply want to compete with a weak hand:

♠ 9 7   ♥ Q 4   ♦ Q J 9 8 6 4   ♣ 6 4

LHO	Partner	RHO	You
	1NT	2♠	2NT
pass	3♣	pass	3♦

Here you want to play undisturbed in 3♦; partner must pass.

Summary

✓ When your partner's 1NT opening is overcalled at the two-level, a Lebensohl relay bid of 2NT forces him to bid 3♣. An immediate double of the overcall is for penalties.

✓ Cuebidding the opponents' suit is Stayman. Bidding 3NT or cuebidding after first bidding the 2NT relay *shows* a stopper in the opponent's suit. Bidding 3NT or cuebidding directly over the overcall *denies* a stopper in the opponents' suit.

✓ With a five-card or longer major suit and a *game-forcing* hand, bid your suit at the three-level immediately. With a six-card minor and an *invitational* hand, bid your suit at the three-level immediately.

✓ Bidding your own suit at the two-level is competitive. If you could have done this, but instead use the 2NT relay and then bid your suit, you are showing an invitational hand. If you have no room to bid your suit at the two-level, bid 2NT. Then if your suit is clubs, pass, otherwise bid your suit, and opener must pass.

LEBENSOHL

What is your next bid on each of the following hands? If you bid 2NT (Lebensohl), what are you going to do next when partner bids 3♣?

1
- ♠ 8
- ♥ Q 8 4
- ♦ 9 7 3
- ♣ K J 8 6 3 2

LHO	Partner	RHO	You
	1NT	2♥	?

2
- ♠ Q J 10 8 6 3
- ♥ 7
- ♦ K 8
- ♣ 9 8 7 4

LHO	Partner	RHO	You
	1NT	2♥	?

3
- ♠ A J 8 4
- ♥ 8
- ♦ A Q 9 7 3 2
- ♣ K 4

LHO	Partner	RHO	You
	1NT	2♥	?

4
- ♠ K Q 7
- ♥ 8 5
- ♦ K J 4 3
- ♣ A J 8 2

LHO	Partner	RHO	You
	1NT	2♥	?

5
- ♠ K Q 3
- ♥ A Q 4
- ♦ J 8 4 2
- ♣ 8 5 3

LHO	Partner	RHO	You
	1NT	2♥	?

6
- ♠ K J 6 3
- ♥ 4
- ♦ A J 6 3
- ♣ J 9 8 4

LHO	Partner	RHO	You
	1NT	2♥	?

7
- ♠ K J 7 4
- ♥ K 5 3
- ♦ 9 8
- ♣ A Q 8 4

LHO	Partner	RHO	You
	1NT	2♥	?

8
- ♠ A J 8
- ♥ J 7 4 3
- ♦ K 8 5
- ♣ 9 7 6

LHO	Partner	RHO	You
	1NT	2♥	?

What is your next bid on each of these hands (playing Lebensohl)?

9
- ♠ A J 7 3
- ♥ 9 7
- ♦ K Q 4
- ♣ A Q 8 3

LHO	Partner	RHO	You
			1NT
2♥	3NT	pass	?

10
- ♠ A K J 3
- ♥ Q 9 7 4
- ♦ Q 7
- ♣ A 9 3

LHO	Partner	RHO	You
			1NT
2♦	3♦	pass	?

ANSWERS

1   2NT   You intend to pass partner's 3♣.

2   2NT   You intend to invite game by bidding 3♠ over partner's 3♣.

3   3♥   You want to reach game and even a slam is not impossible. You start by showing game values and four spades but denying a heart stopper. If partner bids 3NT you can bid 4♦ (which shows slam interest) as you expect 4NT or 5♦ will be safe havens.

4   3NT   This is the hardest one for new Lebensohl players to understand, but when you bid 3NT immediately, partner knows that you do *not* have a heart stopper. As you also do not have four spades, you almost certainly have support for both minors (or a strong minor suit of your own). If partner has no heart stopper either, he will bid his better minor suit and you will reach a minor-suit game, which is very likely to make.

5   2NT   You must be careful not to bid 3NT without thinking. Yes, you almost certainly want to play in 3NT, but if you bid it without first bidding 2NT to show a heart stopper, then partner will remove it when he has no heart stopper. Of course, you will bid 3NT over opener's forced 3♣.

6   3♥   This promises four spades and tells partner that you have nothing in hearts. Perfect!

7   2NT   Over partner's forced 3♣, you plan on bidding 3♥. Now partner will know that you have both four spades and a heart stopper and he will choose the right game.

8   dbl   This is a penalty double. If RHO had passed, then you would have invited game by bidding 2NT. Now you can go for an even bigger score defending 2♥ doubled. Partner will have at least two hearts and you will collect a juicy penalty even when you cannot make game.

9   4♣   Partner doesn't have a heart stopper, so clearly 3NT is not the right contract. He also doesn't have four spades (he would have bid 3♥, not 3NT). Fortunately, you have a nice club suit, for which partner is virtually sure to have decent support.

10   3♥   Partner has no diamond stopper, so 3NT is unlikely to be the right place to play. However, partner has at least one four-card major, so you know you have an eight-card fit somewhere.

REVERSE DRURY

WHAT'S IN A NAME?

♥ In its original form, this convention was devised by **Douglas Drury** *(1914-1967)* of Sebastopol, California, a bridge teacher and club owner. When Drury was living in Toronto, he played with a young Eric Murray who was very fond of super-light third-seat opening bids. Drury devised a convention to avoid getting too high when Murray had opened one of his poorer hands.

When partner opens 1♥ or 1♠ in third or fourth seat, you will frequently have a moderate fit for partner's suit and enough values to invite game. It is quite possible, though, that 2NT or three of partner's major will be too high. This is particularly true after a third-hand opening, when partner may have chosen to open a less than robust hand. **Drury** basically allows you to ask partner if he has a respectable opening bid without committing your side beyond the two-level.

LHO	Partner	RHO	You
			pass
pass	1♥ or 1♠	pass	2♣ (Drury)

A 2♣ response to a third- or fourth-seat major-suit opening is artificial. It shows a maximum pass (a good 10 points or more) and at least three-card support for

BY THE WAY

Most people play that Drury does not apply if the opponent on your right doubles or overcalls partner's opening bid.

partner's major (and preferably four) — in other words, a limit raise of partner's major.

Here's a typical situation:

Partner	You
♠ A Q J 6 4	♠ K 9 3
♥ 7 6 5	♥ K 10 8 4
♦ K 9 3	♦ A J 4
♣ 5 4	♣ 9 7 3

Partner has made a typical 'tactical' 1♠ opening in third chair, and a normal limit raise to 3♠ by you would leave him in a very poor contract. Here is where Drury comes in, since you get to show your hand and still are able to get out at the two-level. Since 2♣ shows support for partner's major, not clubs, it is 100% forcing: *opener may not pass it.*

How do you respond when partner uses Reverse Drury?

LHO	Partner	RHO	You
	pass	pass	1♥
pass	2♣	pass	?

There are four possibilities

2♦ This is a conventional response saying nothing about diamonds. It simply confirms that you have a sound opening bid — i.e. you would have happily opened in first or second chair. Partner can rebid 2♥ now to show a minimum limit raise, or 3♥ to show a maximum passed hand, after which you can make a decision about bidding 4♥.

BY THE WAY

In the original version of the convention, the 2♦ response was used for the poor hand. The modern style is to play Drury as described here, reversing the meanings of the responses — hence the name.

2♥ A sub-minimum opening (not interested in game opposite a limit raise, and may only have four hearts)

4♥ You want to be in game, but have no slam interest

Others There are many ways to play other rebids by opener (new suits at the three-level, notrump rebids, and so), most of which show some slam interest. When you are familiar with the basic convention, you should discuss these sequences with your partner and decide how you want to play them.

After a 1♠ opening bid, the responses are similar, but you have the opportunity to bid a secondary heart suit naturally without going past 2♠, so it makes sense to take advantage of that.

LHO	Partner	RHO	You
	pass	pass	1♠
pass	2♣	pass	?

2♦	Artificial, showing a sound opening bid but denying four hearts
2♥	A full opening bid with at least five spades and at least four hearts
2♠	A sub-minimum opening (not interested in game opposite a limit raise, and may only have four spades)
Others	Very strong hands — see previous comments on this after a 1♥ opening bid.

So now what does a jump raise of partner's major mean?

Playing Drury, all good passed hands with trump support start by bidding 2♣, so the sequences 1♠-3♠ and 1♥-3♥ are no longer needed to show limit raise hands. Jumps to the three-level in partner's major are therefore available for weak, distributional hands with excellent trump support. These are preemptive jumps, similar to those you would make if partner's major-suit opening were doubled for takeout by RHO. You should therefore have four trumps and about 5-8 points to make these bids.

What if you have real clubs?

This is, of course, the drawback to using Drury — you have given up the natural 2♣ response to partner's opening major-suit bid once you are a passed hand. There are two main alternatives, neither of which is really satisfactory.

1. Use 2NT to show about 11-12 HCP, with either a balanced hand or a hand with five clubs that would have responded a natural 2♣.

2. Use a jump to 3♣ to show a hand with six clubs that has about 10-11 HCP, but is too unbalanced to bid notrump comfortably.

Pick your poison!

Summary

✓ Drury only applies when partner opens 1♥ or 1♠ in third or fourth seat and your RHO passes. In this situation, a response of 2♣ is artificial, and shows a limit raise in the major.

✓ The Drury 2♣ bidder promises a maximum pass (10+ points) with at least three-card support for opener's major and preferably four-card support.

✓ Playing Reverse Drury responses, opener rebids his major to show a sub-minimum opening bid.

✓ All other responses, including the artificial 2♦, show a sound opening bid.

✓ A jump raise to three of partner's major is weak and preemptive, since this bid is no longer needed to show a limit raise.

✓ You need to agree with your partner on how to handle hands that would have made a natural 2♣ response.

REVERSE DRURY

NOW TRY THESE...

What is your next bid on each of these auctions (2♣ is Reverse Drury)?

1
- ♠ K 8 3
- ♥ J 8 7 5 3
- ♦ K 7 3
- ♣ 9 2

LHO	Partner	RHO	You
			pass
pass	1♠	pass	?

2
- ♠ A J 8
- ♥ Q 4
- ♦ K J 7 4
- ♣ 9 7 6 4

LHO	Partner	RHO	You
			pass
pass	1♠	pass	?

3
- ♠ K Q 8 4
- ♥ 7
- ♦ A J 9 5
- ♣ 9 7 6 5

LHO	Partner	RHO	You
			pass
pass	1♠	pass	?

4
- ♠ Q 10 8 6 3
- ♥ K 4
- ♦ 3 2
- ♣ 9 7 6 4

LHO	Partner	RHO	You
			pass
pass	1♠	pass	?

5
- ♠ 8
- ♥ K 9 7
- ♦ J 9 8 6
- ♣ K Q 10 8 5

LHO	Partner	RHO	You
			pass
pass	1♠	pass	?

6
- ♠ K Q J 7
- ♥ 9 8
- ♦ A 10 8 5
- ♣ 5 4 2

LHO	Partner	RHO	You
	pass	pass	1♠
pass	2♣	pass	?

7
- ♠ A Q 8 7 3
- ♥ K Q 10 7
- ♦ 4 2
- ♣ A 8

LHO	Partner	RHO	You
	pass	pass	1♠
pass	2♣	pass	?

8
- ♠ A K J 8
- ♥ K Q 9 8 6
- ♦ A Q 2
- ♣ 8

LHO	Partner	RHO	You
	pass	pass	1♥
pass	2♣	pass	?

9
- ♠ K Q 8 4
- ♥ 7 2
- ♦ A J 9 5
- ♣ J 7 5

LHO	Partner	RHO	You
			pass
pass	1♠	pass	2♣
pass	2♦	pass	?

10
- ♠ A J 8
- ♥ K Q 8 4
- ♦ J 7 4 3
- ♣ 6 4

LHO	Partner	RHO	You
			pass
pass	1♠	pass	2♣
pass	2♥	pass	?

ANSWERS

1 2♠ You have a fairly poor hand with spade support; make your normal bid.

2 2♣ Drury. You are maximum with three-card spade support. Perfect.

3 2♣ Drury. Even better — now you have an excellent hand. If partner shows a sound opening bid you intend to go to game and may even show some slam interest.

4 3♠ This is a preemptive raise. Partner will know you have a poor hand with good spade support. Not vulnerable against vulnerable, you might well bid 4♠ with this hand.

5 1NT Of course, you cannot even consider bidding 2♣ on this hand since it shows support for spades. Not that that's any great loss, since venturing to the two-level with a poor hand and no fit for partner is seldom a good idea anyway.

6 2♠ Sometimes, in third seat, you can open a strong four-card major suit, as in this example. Here, you have a sub-minimum opening bid, so just rebid your spades over Drury. Partner will almost certainly pass 2♠ and, as he will have at least three-card (and often four-card) support, this will be a sensible contract.

7 2♥ This confirms that you have a sound opening bid. With a weak hand you always rebid your major.

8 2♠ This shows a normal reverse (i.e. a strong hand with at least five hearts and at least four spades). This is easy to remember — with a weak hand you never go beyond two of the major for which partner has shown support. With this hand you are too good to bid a simple 4♥ over a Drury 2♣ as you might easily have a slam even opposite a passed partner.

9 4♠ Partner has shown a sound opening bid; opposite that, you can re-evaluate your hand to an opening bid in support of spades, so raise to game.

10 4♥ Partner's 2♥ bid shows a full opening bid. Your 2♣ bid told partner that you had three spades, so now show that you have four hearts and a super-maximum for your initial pass. If you have a choice, it is usually better to play in a 4-4 major-suit fit rather than a 5-3, since the five-card suit can often be used for discards.

CHAPTER 20

ROMAN KEY CARD BLACKWOOD

WHAT'S IN A NAME?

♥A modern variation of the Blackwood convention, Roman Key Card Blackwood (RKC) was first widely publicized by **Eddie Kantar** of Santa Monica, California. This convention is still developing and growing, as evidenced by the recent publication of the 3rd edition of Kantar's book *Roman Key Card Blackwood, Slam Bidding in the 21st Century*.

Just like the original Blackwood, RKC was devised not to help you get to more slams but to keep you out of bad ones! Go back and read that sentence as many times as you wish. It is one of the keys to successful slam bidding. In addition to asking about aces, RKC also allows you to find out whether partner has either or both of the king and queen of trumps. Because partner includes these cards in his response, you must have an agreed trump suit before you can invoke RKC. If there is *any* doubt which suit is agreed for purposes of counting key cards, then the last-bid suit is the key suit.

You've probably bid the occasional slam with a trump suit like A10874 opposite 9653. When the trumps broke

BY THE WAY

All the rules we gave back in Chapter 6 for using simple Blackwood still apply. Before reading this chapter, you are advised to go back and review the earlier discussion. We would also suggest that you make sure you are confident that you understand the simple version before you attempt to play Roman Key Card (hereafter called simply RKC).

3-1 (as expected) and you lost two trump tricks, all you could say to partner was: 'That was unlucky, but I had no way to find out if you had the king'.

At least in this example trumps might have broken 2-2. Even more embarrassing is when your trumps are Q10853 opposite partner's J964. Now you are bound to lose two tricks no matter how the opponents' trumps are divided. What's more, if one opponent has both the ace and the king he will probably double you to add insult to injury. Well, thanks to RKC, there is a way to stay out of such poor slams.

How does RKC work?

Instead of just counting the aces in your hand, you will now pretend that there is a fifth ace... the king of trumps. The four aces and the trump king are called **key cards**. As long as you can count to five, you can manage this convention. It begins in the familiar manner, with a 4NT bid:

Partner	You
1♥	3♥
4NT	?

Here is how you respond:

5♣	1 or 4 key cards
5♦	3 or 0 key cards
5♥	2 or 5 key cards *without* the queen of trumps
5♠	2 or 5 key cards *with* the queen of trumps

BY THE WAY

When you meet and play with others who also play RKC, you will discover that there are two schemes of responses. We recommend playing 5♣=1/4 and 5♦=0/3. This version of RKC is called '1430'. However, it is equally workable to switch the meanings of these two responses ('0314') and if you prefer to do so, that is okay. Just be sure that you and your partner agree which version you are playing.

That is not too tough to remember. You know the score for making a vulnerable 6♥ or 6♠ at duplicate — 1430. If you can remember that, you can remember the meaning of the 5♣ and 5♦ RKC responses — 5♣ = 1/4 (1 or 4 key cards) and 5♦ = 3/0. Notice, too, the use of the 5♥ and 5♠ responses to give information about the trump queen.

Are you thinking, 'How do I know whether partner has one key card or four?' After looking at your hand and thinking about the previous bidding, if you do not know which partner has then you should not have been asking about key cards. Trust us when we say that *if* you have a Blackwood bid you can always work out the meaning of the response.

Playing RKC, you will never get to a small slam missing two key cards (one missing is OK) and never get to a grand slam missing any key card. Yes, it is true that this way you will also not get to a slam that depends on a finesse for the king of trumps, but this is not such a bad thing in the long run. If you can avoid any slam that needs a finesse you will be a consistent winner on these hands. (Slams 'on a finesse' are never really 50% since bad trump breaks, defensive ruffs, and similar unpleasant things tend to scupper them too).

Asking for kings

Just as when you use ordinary Blackwood, you can continue with 5NT after the initial RKC response to ask partner how many kings he has. This applies no matter which response partner gave to the RKC enquiry. Since you have already counted the king of trumps, do not show it again; just respond as you would to regular Blackwood, but only count kings outside the trump suit.

Asking about the queen of trumps

When partner responds 5♥ or 5♠ to your RKC 4NT he immediately tells you whether or not he has the queen of trumps. When he responds 5♣ or 5♦, he does not. You therefore need a second asking bid to discover that information. Once you know how many key cards are missing, perhaps you want to bid a slam (or a grand slam) only if partner has the queen to solidify the trumps.

Read this next sentence two or three times until you are sure you understand it. After the first RKC response, *the lowest available bid that is not your agreed suit asks about the trump queen.* Do you want to go back and read that one more time? We'll wait right here for you.

Okay. Ready to proceed? So, after you bid 4NT, if partner responds 5♣, 5♦ asks about the queen *except* when diamonds is your agreed suit, when 5♥ asks. If partner responds 5♦ to your 4NT, 5♥ asks about the queen *except* when hearts is your agreed suit, when 5♠ asks. These bids are called the **queen ask**. If you did not understand that, go back and read it again.

How do you respond to the queen ask?

The *lowest available* bid in the agreed trump suit *denies* the queen of trumps (this will usually be at the five-level, but may be at the six-level). It will obviously never be a jump bid. This bid says nothing else about your hand other than, 'I do not have the queen of trumps'.

Any other bid *promises* the queen of trumps. A *jump* in the agreed trump suit shows the queen of trumps but denies an outside king. A bid of a suit other than the trump suit shows the queen of trumps and the king of the bid suit. (As when cuebidding, you bid your lowest king if you have more than one). However, you may not bid higher than six of the agreed suit. If you have the queen of trumps and a higher-ranking king, bid 5NT.

An example auction:

Partner	You
1♥	3♥
4NT	5♦[1]
5♠[2]	6♦[3]
7♥[4]	

1) 0 or 3 key cards
2) Queen ask (hearts is the agreed suit)
3) Heart queen and diamond king, denies club king
4) That's what I wanted to know!

Summary

✓ *All* the rules that applied to using Blackwood in Chapter 6 still apply.

✓ There are five key cards — the four aces plus the king of the agreed trump suit.

✓ If there is *any* doubt which suit is agreed, the last-bid suit should be considered the key suit for purposes of counting key cards.

✓ Responder bids 5♣ with 1 or 4 key cards, 5♦ with 0 or 3 key cards, 5♥ with 2 (or 5) key cards but no queen of trumps, 5♠ with 2 (or 5) key cards and the queen of trumps.

✓ 5NT by the RKC bidder asks how many of the three non-trump kings partner has (use regular Blackwood responses).

✓ The next non-trump step after a 5♣/5♦ response asks about the queen of trumps. Responder signs off at the lowest level in the trump suit if he does not have it. Holding the trump queen, responder cuebids his lowest-ranking outside king, or jumps in the trump suit with no outside kings, or bids 5NT if cuebidding his lowest outside king would mean going past six of your agreed trump suit.

ROMAN KEY CARD BLACKWOOD

NOW TRY THESE...

What is your next bid on each of these auctions? In each case, assume hearts have been agreed as trumps in the unseen auction that precedes the (RKC) 4NT

1
♠ A 8
♥ K Q 8 3
♦ J 9 6 3
♣ K 4

Partner	You
4NT	? *5S*

2
♣ A 9 4
♥ A Q 4 2
♦ A 10 7 3
♣ A 5

Partner	You
4NT	? *5♣*

3
♠ K Q 6 3
♥ K 6 3
♦ K J 8 7 5
♣ 3

Partner	You
4NT	? *5C*

4
♠ K Q 6 3
♥ K 6 3
♦ K J 8 7 5
♣ 3

Partner	You
4NT	5♣
5♦	? *5H*

5
♠ A 9 4
♥ A Q 4 2
♦ A 10 7 3
♣ A 5

Partner	You
4NT	5♣
5♦	? *6H*

6
♠ Q 8
♥ K Q 8 3
♦ J 9 6 3
♣ K 4 2

Partner	You
4NT	5♣
5♦	? *6C*

7
♠ A Q 6 3
♥ K 6 3
♦ A J 8 7 5
♣ 3

Partner	You
4NT	5♦
5♥	? *P*

8
♠ K Q 6 3
♥ Q 3 2
♦ Q J 8 7 5
♣ 3

Partner	You
4NT	5♦
5♠	? *5N*

ANSWERS

1 5♠ You have two key cards (♠A and ♥K) plus the queen of trumps.

2 5♣ You have four key cards. 5♣ = 1 or 4.

3 5♣ You have one key card (♥K). 5♣ = 1 or 4.

4 5♥ You do not have the queen of trumps (hearts) so you make the lowest available bid in the agreed suit.

5 6♥ You have the queen of trumps but no outside king, so you jump in the agreed suit.

6 6♣ You have the queen of trumps and an outside king. Cuebidding your (lowest) king also shows the ♥Q.

7 pass 5♥ was a sign off. 5♠ would have asked for the trump queen.

8 5NT You have the queen of trumps and an outside king. However, cuebidding your ♠K would take you past 6♥. Bidding 5NT show the ♥Q as well as a king too high-ranking to cuebid.

FOURTH-SUIT FORCING

WHAT'S IN A NAME?

♥Although the convention is now universally known as Fourth-Suit Forcing (FSF for short) this is, in fact, a misnomer since everyone would play a bid of the fourth suit as forcing. The convention was originally called 'Fourth-Suit Artificial', which is a much more accurate description. The method was first introduced by English expert *Norman Squire (1907-1991)*.

Partner	You	
1♠	2♦	
2♥	3♣	*(fourth-suit forcing)*

When three suits have been bid, if responder bids the fourth suit at his second turn, it is an artificial bid saying nothing about his holding in the suit bid, but simply creating a game force. The basic message it sends to partner is, 'I have enough values to play in game, but I do not know yet where we should play the hand'. Basically, bidding the fourth suit asks opener to describe his hand further.

As you will see, once responder uses 'Fourth-Suit Forcing' (hereafter referred to as FSF) you are in a game-forcing auction. Neither partner may pass until at least game is reached.

Why would you use Fourth-Suit Forcing?

There is one sequence where a bid
of the fourth suit is not FSF:

1♣   1♦
1♥   1♠

Here the 1♠ bid is natural (and still
forcing, but only for one round).
After the auction begins 1♣-1♦-
1♥-? a jump to 2♠ is FSF.
However, some players still like to
use 1♠ here as the
artificial bid.

1. You have a notrump-oriented hand with no stopper in the unbid suit.

♠ K Q 7 3   ♥ A 5   ♦ A 6 4 3   ♣ 10 8 4

Partner	You
1♥	1♠
2♦	?

Clearly, you want to play in game — but which one? You cannot rebid your four-card spade suit, and partner may not be impressed if you jump to 4♥ with only a doubleton in trumps. You cannot bid 3♦ as that would be non-forcing — besides, if partner has a minimum opening bid it is unlikely that you will have enough power to make an eleven-trick game. It is much more likely that 3NT is the right spot; however, you can hardly bid 3NT with three baby clubs. More to the point, if partner's clubs are something like ♣Kx wouldn't it be better for him to play the notrump?

This is a perfect hand on which to use FSF, as you have no clear-cut bid. Essentially, you want to know if partner has a club stopper. You bid 3♣ in the hope that he will bid 3NT once he knows you have the values to insist on game.

2. You don't know which game to bid

♠ K Q 9 8 5   ♥ A 7 3   ♦ K 5   ♣ Q 7 4

Partner	You
1♦	1♠
2♣	?

Again, you want to play in game, and without FSF available, you would probably jump to 3NT. However, this is unlikely to produce the desired outcome if partner produces a 3-1-5-4 hand and the opponents remove your only heart stopper at trick one. No, if partner has three-card spade support then 4♠ is almost certain to be a much better spot. Employing FSF gives partner room to support your spades if he has a three-card fit with you, so bid 2♥.

These two examples represent the most frequent reasons for using FSF. However, the third application is the one that produces the greatest benefit:

3. Conserving space in a potential slam auction

♠ A Q 8 5   ♥ K 5 4   ♦ K 9   ♣ A J 7 4

Partner	You
1♦	1♠
2♣	?

Your hand keeps getting better and better. First, partner opened the bidding, and now he has bid a suit for which you have good four-card support. You smell a slam, and perhaps even a grand slam. How should you proceed?

You cannot bid 3♣, as that would not be forcing. You could jump to 4♣, but that uses up an awful lot of valuable space that you will need to investigate slam prospects fully. As you will have guessed, the answer is to wheel out FSF. When you bid 2♥, partner will probably bid 2♠ or 2NT. Then you can bid a forcing 3♣ and partner will know you have slam interest.

BY THE WAY

You may also want to rebid your own suit below 3NT without risking partner's passing. Once again, you can achieve this by using FSF first.

What do you do when partner uses FSF?

Simple — describe your hand further. Your first priority is to show delayed support for responder's first suit, as in the second example above. The second consideration is to show a stopper in the fourth suit by bidding notrump. If you do not have a hand that enables you to do either of these things, make the most descriptive bid available. Be warned, you will occasionally be stuck:

♠ 6 4　♥ J 5　♦ K Q J 8 5　♣ A Q 10 3

You	Partner
1♦	1♠
2♣	2♥
?	

BY THE WAY

FSF no longer applies if either of you is a passed hand.

Yuk! You cannot support partner's spades with only a doubleton, nor can you tell partner you have a heart stopper when you hold only ♥Jx. Obviously, you will have to rebid one of your suits. If you bid 3♣, then partner will think you are 5-5, and if you bid 3♦ then it sounds like you have a 6-4 shape. The least of evils is to rebid your better minor (3♦ in this case). Remember, also, that partner is aware that you may be in this position.

What do you do when you actually have the fourth suit?

You will rarely want to play in the fourth suit. Even though you may have four cards in that suit, it will seldom produce an eight-card fit. Indeed, in many auctions, partner cannot hold as much as four-card support. For example:

♠ K 4　♥ K J 9 4　♦ A J 8 6 3　♣ Q 7

Partner	You
1♣	1♦
1♠	?

Partner would have bid hearts before spades holding four of each, so there's no need to worry about how to suggest hearts as a potential trump suit. You *have* good hearts, so just bid 3NT. Contrast that with this hand on the same auction:

♠ K 8 3   ♥ 9 6   ♦ A K J 7 3   ♣ A 7 3

This time, it is far from certain what the right contract will be. Notrump is unattractive because you *do not* have good hearts, so bid FSF — 2♥.

When as responder you have a strong (game-going) two-suited hand, it is quite possible (even likely) that by the time you get to bid a second time your second suit will be the fourth suit. For example:

♠ A Q 9 8 5 3   ♥ 4   ♦ A K J 9 5   ♣ 3

Partner	You
1♥	1♠
2♣	?

What a surprise — partner has hearts and clubs. Anything could be the best spot — 3NT, 4♠, 4♥ or even 7♦. Asking partner to describe his hand is not likely to help you much — he will not support spades with only ♠Kx, nor will he bid notrump with only ♦Qx. No, if you bid 2♦ (FSF) partner is almost certain to rebid one of his suits and you still will not know if he has a 1-6-1-5 shape or a 2-5-2-4 hand. In these circumstances, it is much better to describe your hand to partner, and you can still do so even playing FSF. If you *jump* in the fourth suit at your second turn to call, that shows a two-suiter (at least 5-5 and probably more) and at least the values for game. This hand is perfect for a jump to 3♦.

Summary

✓ A bid of the fourth suit at responder's second turn is artificial (FSF) and establishes a game-forcing situation.

✓ After 1♣-1♦-1♥-? a bid of 1♠ is natural and forcing only one round, while a bid of 2♠ is game-forcing and artificial.

✓ In all other situations, a jump in the fourth suit at responder's second turn shows a game-going two-suited hand, at least 5-5.

✓ In response to FSF, opener describes his hand by supporting responder's first suit (with three cards in that suit), bidding no-trump with a stopper in the fourth suit or, lacking the ability to do either of the above, rebids one of his own suits.

FOURTH-SUIT FORCING

NOW TRY THESE...

What is your next bid on each of these hands?

1   ♠   A 5
    ♥   9 5 3
    ♦   K 8 4
    ♣   A Q 8 6 4

Partner	You
1♠	2♣
2♦	?

2   ♠   K 4
    ♥   Q 7 5
    ♦   J 8 3
    ♣   A K J 8 5

Partner	You
1♠	2♣
2♥	?

3   ♠   K 3
    ♥   A 4
    ♦   8 7
    ♣   A Q J 8 5 4 3

Partner	You
1♠	2♣
2♦	?

4   ♠   A Q 8 5
    ♥   K 7
    ♦   A Q J 8 5
    ♣   A 7

Partner	You
1♣	1♦
1♠	?

5   ♠   K Q 9 8 6
    ♥   K 5
    ♦   A 8 4
    ♣   Q 7 4

Partner	You
1♥	1♠
2♣	?

6   ♠   K Q 8 6
    ♥   K 7
    ♦   8 6 3
    ♣   A J 10 8

Partner	You
1♥	1♠
2♦	?

7   ♠   9 6 3
    ♥   K 7 4
    ♦   K Q 8 5
    ♣   A Q 7

Partner	You
1♣	1♦
1♥	?

8   ♠   A Q J 9 7
    ♥   K J 6
    ♦   Q 7
    ♣   9 6 3

Partner	You
1♥	1♠
2♦	?

9   ♠   A J 6
    ♥   A 6 3
    ♦   7 5
    ♣   A Q J 9 7

Partner	You
1♠	2♣
2♦	?

10   ♠   7
    ♥   A Q J 8 6
    ♦   3 2
    ♣   A K 6 4 3

Partner	You
1♦	1♥
1♠	?

ANSWERS

1   **2♥**   It seems likely that 3NT will be the best contract if partner has a heart stopper. If he does not, then you will have to look for an alternative spot. FSF should uncover this information.

2   **3♦**   You have no way to guess the right final contract. Consult partner by using FSF.

3   **2♥**   This time, you have a heart stopper, but it is far from clear that 3NT is the best spot. Indeed, even 7♣ could be cold, but you would rather not commit to bypassing the notrump game yet. You cannot bid 3♣ now as that would be non-forcing and you certainly want to make sure of reaching game. Use FSF now and you should be able to make a forcing 3♣ bid next time.

4   **4NT**   Yes, you can get very technical here and start a delicate sequence with 2♥ (FSF) but why bother? Especially if you're playing the Roman Key Card version, Blackwood is going to give you all the information you need to decide whether to play 6♠ or 7♠. Remember that if no suit has been explicitly agreed, a jump to 4NT sets the last-bid suit as trumps — in this case, spades.

5   **2♦**   You could jump to 3NT, and that may well be the final contract, but you should use FSF first in case partner has three-card spade support.

6   **3NT**   You could bid 3♣ FSF, but why do that? What would you hope to achieve? You already know that you want to play in game, you have no fit, and you have no worries about the unbid suit.

7   **2♠**   'I have the values for game but need help in spades...' — the perfect message to send!

8   **4♥**   You have already found your eight-card (or better) major-suit fit, so why bother with FSF? Show both the values for game and the heart fit now and leave any further move to partner.

9   **2♥**   Similar to the previous hand in that you know which suit you want to be trumps (spades in this case), but this time you are too strong to make a limited bid. You need to conserve space on this hand. Start with 2♥ intending to set spades as trumps on the next round, and leaving lots of room to explore the right level.

10   **3♣**   A strong two-suiter in hearts and clubs. Perfect!

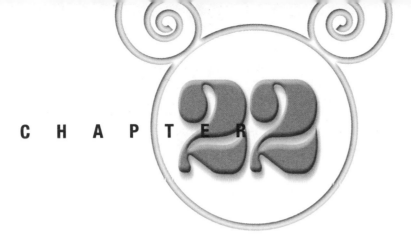

CHAPTER 22

NEW MINOR FORCING

WHAT'S IN A NAME?

New Minor Forcing originated in two earlier conventions which had a similar purpose. They are Checkback Stayman (used in North America) and Crowhurst (developed by *Eric Crowhurst* of Reading, England) which is very popular in the U.K.

Playing standard methods, your second bid *over partner's 1NT rebid* in each of the following auctions would be considered non-forcing:

	Partner	You
	1♣	1♠
	1NT	2♦

or

	Partner	You
	1♦	1♠
	1NT	2♥

In each case, your actions show a weak two-suited hand and partner may pass at this point if he prefers your second suit. Very convenient — *if* you have a weak two-suiter. However, what this means is that whenever you have a game-going hand you must leap about. Obviously, jumping the bidding uses up valuable space, and that is not ideal either when you want to investigate which game to play or when you have slam interest.

Playing **New Minor Forcing** (hereafter called NMF) a bid of a previously unbid minor suit over a 1NT rebid is artificial (something like Fourth-Suit Forcing), and asks opener to describe his hand further. Thus, after:

Partner	You
1♣	1♥ or 1♠
1NT	?

2♦ is artificial and forcing, while 2♣ is to play.

Partner	You
1♦	1♥ or 1♠
1NT	?

Here, 2♣ is artificial and forcing while 2♦ is to play.

What do you need to use NMF?

Responder guarantees at least enough values to invite game facing the 1NT rebid, so a minimum of 11 HCP. By far the most common reason for using NMF is that you have a five-card major and would like to know whether partner has three-card support. Let's say you have:

♠ A K 8 5 3　♥ K 6 4　♦ 8 4　♣ A 8 3

Partner	You
1♣	1♠
1NT	?

Clearly, you want to play in game. Do you think you should bid 3NT or 4♠? Of course, there is no correct answer to this question. However, in traditional methods there is no sensible way to find out if partner has three-card spade support. Playing NMF you bid the unbid minor (2♦) and he will tell you.

♠ A K 8 5 3　♥ 9 6 4　♦ 8 4　♣ A 8 3

Partner	You
1♣	1♠
1NT	?

This time you have an additional problem — is partner maximum or minimum for his 1NT rebid? You could make an invitational raise to 2NT, but if opener has a minimum he will pass and you will play in 2NT even when he has three-card support for your suit and a spade partscore would be a much safer spot. Once again, using NMF (2♦) is the answer since partner will not only tell you about his spade support, but also whether he has a maximum hand.

Can you use NMF when you have both majors?

You certainly can. Indeed, hands with five spades and four or more hearts can be bid much more accurately using NMF. Consider this problem playing traditional methods:

♠ AK853   ♥ KJ64   ♦ 84   ♣ K3

Partner	You
1♣	1♠
1NT	?

Playing NMF, you start by bidding 2♦, your artificial forcing bid. Remember, this bid asks partner to describe his hand further. If he has four hearts he will tell you about them. If he does not, you need never bid the suit. Easy! As a result, when you jump to 3♥ in this auction rather than using NMF, you guarantee a five-card suit. With a weak hand, and four or more hearts, you simply bid 2♥. Partner now has a lot of information with which to make a decision on how high to bid, and in which denomination.

What if both minors are unbid?

There is only one auction that can produce this situation:

♠ AJ864   ♥ Q6   ♦ KJ6   ♣ 963

Partner	You
1♥	1♠
1NT	?

Treat a bid of either minor as semi-artificial and forcing for one round. Bid your better minor (usually the minor in which you have a notrump stopper) — on this hand, bid 2♦. Partner will tell you if he has 3-card spade support and whether he is maximum for his 1NT rebid. He will also know to avoid 3NT if he also has weak clubs. If your minors were reversed, you would bid 2♣ instead.

What do you do when partner uses NMF?

Having looked at the various problems from responder's side of the table, we now move around to opener's seat. You open the bidding and rebid 1NT. Partner now wheels out his new toy — New Minor Forcing. What do you do? The responses to NMF convey a considerable amount of information regarding shape and strength. They are listed here in order of priority.

Priority 1: Show an unbid four-card major.

This can only be hearts — if you had four spades you would have rebid 1♠ rather than 1NT. Note that you will often have four hearts when you open a minor and rebid 1NT over partner's 1♠ response. You have neither the shape nor the

BY THE WAY

There are many other possible bidding structures over NMF, some of which do not involve jump rebids by opener.

strength to reverse, so you had to settle for 1NT. Now partner asks for more information:

♠ K 3   ♥ K J 8 5   ♦ A J 8 4   ♣ Q 8 4

You	Partner
1♦	1♠
1NT	2♣
?	

How many hearts do you bid? As is the case in all of the replies to NMF, you make the minimum bid with a minimum hand, and jump with a maximum. The hand above has 14 points, so you would jump to 3♥. (We are calling this hand a maximum because your 1NT rebid shows 12-14 HCP.)

Remember that when he uses NMF partner only promises the values to invite game (11 points). He also knows that you may have only 12 points. 11+12 does not sound like enough points for game, so you must jump to show your full-strength opening bid when you are a little better than minimum. If you had a minimum opening bid with four hearts, you would rebid 2♥ only.

Priority 2: Support partner's suit if you can.

♠ K 7 5   ♥ A 6 2   ♦ K J 8 5   ♣ K 8 5

You	Partner
1♦	1♠
1NT	2♣
?	

Partner bids 2♣, NMF, over your 1NT rebid. You do not have four hearts, so you can ignore Priority 1. Priority 2 is to show support for partner's suit, which you have here. As before, you are maximum for your 12-14 1NT rebid, so you must jump to show this too — bid 3♠. With the same shape and a minimum opener you would simply bid 2♠.

Priority 3: Show your range.

If you do not have an unbid heart suit and cannot support partner, the only thing left to show is your range — maximum or minimum. When you have a minimum hand, you have two options:

♠ 8 6   ♥ A Q 7   ♦ K 10 9 7 5   ♣ K 10 6

You	Partner
1♦	1♠
1NT	2♣
?	

You do not have four hearts and you cannot support spades. You have a minimum opening bid with stoppers in the two unbid suits (remember that partner's 2♣ bid was artificial, so only diamonds and spades have been bid naturally). Bid 2NT. If partner has only invitational values, he will pass. If he bids again then you are now in a game-forcing auction.

♠ K 6   ♥ A Q 7   ♦ K 10 9 7 5   ♣ 10 8 6

You	Partner
1♦	1♠
1NT	2♣
?	

As before, you do not have four hearts and you cannot support spades. You again have a minimum opening bid, but this time you have no stopper in one of the unbid suits, clubs. Rebid your first suit — bid 2♦. If partner has only invitational values he will either pass or convert to 2NT. Any other continuation creates a game-forcing auction. Given the chance, you can bid the suit in which you have a stopper.

When you have a maximum, you must force to game since you know that partner has at least an invitational hand. Essentially, you can make any bid that we have not so far mentioned, but you have two basic choices:

♠ Q 6   ♥ A Q 7   ♦ K 10 9 7 5   ♣ K 10 6

This is the same hand as before, but with the ♠Q added to make it a maximum 1NT rebid. You still do not have four hearts, nor can you support spades. However, with stoppers in the unbid suits and a maximum you can bid 3NT.

♠ K 6   ♥ 10 8 6   ♦ K Q 9 7 5   ♣ A Q 7

This time you have a maximum with a stopper in only one of the unbid suits. How you show this will depend on which suits have previously been bid. On the auction above, you can simply show your stopper by bidding the suit you have stopped — 3♣. This cannot be a natural bid since you did not bid 2♣ at your second turn.

♠ K 6   ♥ A Q 7   ♦ K Q 9 7 5   ♣ 10 8 6

Now you cannot bid the suit in which you have a stopper — hearts — as that would show the suit. The answer is to jump in your first suit — 3♦ — to show extra values but a hand that cannot bid 3NT or 3♣. Partner will work out why.

What do you do when you don't have enough to invite to game?

Let's start with the simple situation:

♠ K Q 8 6 3   ♥ Q 10 8 3   ♦ 8 5   ♣ 7 2

Partner	You
1♣	1♠
1NT	?

Clearly, facing a 12-14 HCP hand, you have no interest in game. Since your second suit is hearts, you can just go ahead and bid it — 2♥. Not only does this tell partner you are at least 5-4 in the majors (with 4-4 you would have responded

1♥ not 1♠) but it also tells him not to bid too much. His choices are simple — pass 2♥ or give preference to 2♠.

We know what you're thinking — 'What about when my second suit is an unbid minor?' You don't really want to play in 1NT when you hold a hand like this one:

♠ K 10 6 3   ♥ 8 4   ♦ 9   ♣ Q J 9 7 5 3

Partner	You
1♦	1♠
1NT	?

You are fairly sure that clubs will play at least as well as notrump and probably much better. However, you do not have the values to invite game, so you cannot bid 2♣ as that would be NMF. What a nasty situation.

The solution is that you can jump to 3♣. This says to partner, 'Please pass and put down dummy'. Note that as partner cannot pass a 2♣ bid, you no longer need 3♣ as a forcing bid.

Summary

✓ A bid of an unbid minor after a 1NT rebid is artificial and guarantees at least the values to invite game. Opener describes his hand in terms of shape and strength.

✓ When both minors are unbid, bid your stronger minor as NMF.

✓ A jump by responder in an unbid minor after a 1NT rebid is weak and to play.

✓ Over NMF. opener must show an unbid heart suit if he has four of them.

✓ Failing that, opener must show three-card support for responder's suit if he can.

✓ Opener bids notrump, rebids his suit or shows stoppers (with a maximum) when he can fulfill neither of the first two priorities.

NEW MINOR FORCING

NOW TRY THESE...

What is your next bid on each of these hands?

1
- ♠ K J 8 5 3
- ♥ A 8 6 4
- ♦ 8
- ♣ K Q 5

Partner	You
1♣	1♠
1NT	?

2
- ♠ K Q 10 7 5 3
- ♥ A 7
- ♦ J 8
- ♣ 9 7 5

Partner	You
1♣	1♠
1NT	?

3
- ♠ K Q 9 5 3
- ♥ A J 8 5
- ♦ J 6
- ♣ K 5

Partner	You
1♦	1♠
1NT	?

4
- ♠ K Q 9 6
- ♥ A J 8 5
- ♦ J 6
- ♣ K Q 5

Partner	You
1♦	1♥
1NT	?

5
- ♠ K J 8 5 3
- ♥ J 7
- ♦ A Q 5
- ♣ 9 6 3

Partner	You
1♥	1♠
1NT	?

6
- ♠ K 9 6 4
- ♥ 7
- ♦ Q J 9 6 4 2
- ♣ 9 5

Partner	You
1♥	1♠
1NT	?

7
- ♠ K J 6
- ♥ J 9 7 4
- ♦ A 5
- ♣ K Q 7 2

Partner	You
	1♣
1♠	1NT
2♦	?

8
- ♠ 8 6 4
- ♥ A K 7
- ♦ Q J 7 4
- ♣ K 10 5

Partner	You
	1♦
1♠	1NT
2♣	?

9
- ♠ K Q 4
- ♥ A 7
- ♦ Q J 10 8 3
- ♣ 9 6 3

Partner	You
	1♦
1♥	1NT
2♣	?

10
- ♠ K Q 4
- ♥ A 7
- ♦ A J 10 8 5
- ♣ 9 6 3

Partner	You
	1♦
1♥	1NT
2♣	?

ANSWERS

1 2♦   You have invitational (or better) values but you cannot yet tell which is the best game. Ask partner to tell you more about his hand.

2 3♠   This time you can describe your hand by making an invitational jump rebid of your own suit. If you use NMF and partner rebids 2NT to show a minimum without three spades, you can no longer stop in 3♠ as that would now be a forcing bid. You will only have two choices, both poor — pass 2NT or force to game.

3 2♣   3NT, 4♥ and 4♠ are all possible contracts at this point. You need more information. By using NMF you will find out whether partner has a fit with your second suit — he will bid hearts if he has four of them. If he does not, he will support spades if he has three of those. Whatever partner does next, you will be well placed to select the correct game contract.

4 3NT   Where else are you going on this hand? Partner cannot have four spades as he did not bid 1♠ at his second turn. You do not really care whether or not he has three hearts, nor does it matter whether he is minimum or maximum. Bidding NMF on this hand will just give free information about partner's hand to the defenders.

5 2♦   You want to find out whether partner has three-card spade support and whether he is maximum or minimum. As there are two unbid minors, choose the one in which you have more strength.

6 3♦   You do not want to pass 1NT, but you cannot bid 2♦ as that would be NMF. Jumping to 3♦ tells partner to pass. This should be at least as good a spot as 1NT and will frequently be much better.

7 3♥   Your first priority is to show four hearts. Since you have a maximum for your 12-14 point 1NT rebid, you must also jump.

8 2♠   You do not have four hearts to show, but you do have three-card support for partner's spades. With a minimum opening bid, you therefore support spades at the cheapest available level.

9 2♦   You have no unbid major to show, and you do not have support for partner's suit. You also have a minimum opening bid. You would bid 2NT if you had stoppers in both unbid suits (spades and clubs) but with no club stopper you simply rebid your suit.

10 2♠   The same type of hand as in Question 9 but this time a maximum. With stoppers in both black suits, you would jump to 3NT, but lacking a club stopper you show all of the features of your hand by bidding your spade stopper now. Note that 2♠ cannot show a four-card suit as you did not bid 1♠ over partner's 1♥ response.

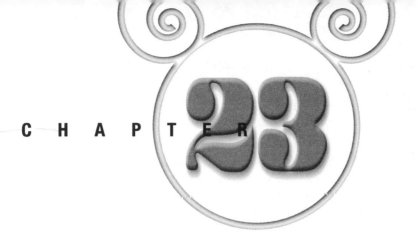

OGUST RESPONSES
TO WEAK TWO-BIDS

You will recall that in Chapter 3 we introduced Weak Two-Bids. At that point, we suggested that when partner bids 2NT to enquire about your hand you should respond by showing any high-card feature outside your long suit. That is a workable method, and one played by many leading pairs. However, if you want to get a little more fancy you might try adopting the **Ogust** method of rebidding over the 2NT enquiry.

Playing Ogust, the meaning of each rebid is the same regardless of whether proceedings began with a Weak Two-Bid in diamonds, in hearts or in spades. The responses take the form of a series of steps, starting at 3♣, each one conveying specific information about the quality of opener's suit, and whether or not he is minimum or maximum for his Weak Two opening bid. Among other advantages, this allows you to be somewhat more frisky with the hands on which you are prepared to open a Weak Two, especially at favorable vulnerability. In other words, your Weak Two can be *really* weak if you want!

You	**Partner**
2♦, 2♥, 2♠	2NT
?	

Ogust rebids by opener over 2NT

3♣	minimum points, poor suit
3♦	minimum points, good suit
3♥	maximum points, poor suit
3♠	maximum points, good suit
3NT	solid suit

BY THE WAY

In the original Ogust scheme the 3♦ and 3♥ bids were reversed. A few players still play the convention this way, but the responses as listed here are those most commonly used.

Each of these bids is wholly artificial, and says nothing about the suit actually bid.

Why play Ogust rebids?

When we first introduced Weak Two's, we said that the opener always promised a good suit — at least two of the top three honors, or three of the top five. A Weak Two-Bid also has a fairly narrow HCP range (usually 5-9 or 6-10). Combining this narrow range with the suit-quality restriction means that classic Weak Two's occur relatively infrequently.

However, many players really enjoy making life tough for the opponents with preemptive bids, and a Weak Two is really just a low-level preempt. In order to increase the frequency of Weak Two's, they allow opener more latitude regarding suit quality. We would not recommend opening a Weak Two with a suit of Q97643 when vulnerable, but not vulnerable you can cause severe problems for the opponents by doing so, with relatively little risk to your side.

Of course, sometimes it is the partner of the Weak Two opener who has the good hand. If opener might have either AKJ863 or Q97643 for his Weak Two, then responder needs a way to find out which it is. After all, when responder has a strong hand it will often be the quality of opener's long suit that determines whether the hand belongs in 3NT or in game in opener's suit. This is where Ogust rebids come in.

When do you show a 'good' suit?

Playing Ogust rebids, you show a good suit when you have a classic Weak Two — two of the top three honors not vulnerable, and a little better than that vulnerable. With weaker holdings, you show a poor suit. For example, when non-vulnerable, you would describe KQ8753 as a 'good suit'. Vulnerable, you would treat such a holding as a 'poor suit', but describe KQ10953 as 'good'. Exactly where the line is drawn must be determined by how 'loose' (or 'random') your partnership elects to play its Weak Two openings. Obviously, at any vulnerability, you would describe any suit headed by AKQ as 'solid' and rebid 3NT.

What happens after partner rebids?

Obviously you can pass, if partner's Ogust response happens to repeat his suit. More often, opposite a minimum, you will sign off in partner's suit at the three-level. You may also bid 3NT (which partner should pass) or jump to game in partner's suit. Finally, if you are interested in slam, you can introduce a new suit, which would be a cuebid agreeing partner's suit. (If you have a strong suit of your own, you bid it immediately without using the 2NT enquiry).

Summary

✓ After opening a Weak Two-Bid and hearing a strong 2NT enquiry, opener uses artificial step responses to show two things: minimum or maximum hand, and a bad or good suit.

✓ What your partnership decides to define as a 'good' suit will depend on the latitude you are going to allow for a Weak Two.

✓ Since immediate bids of new suits are forcing, if responder bids 2NT first and then introduces a new suit over opener's rebid, that bid is a cuebid agreeing opener's suit and suggesting slam.

OGUST RESPONSES TO WEAK TWO-BIDS

NOW TRY THESE...

What is your next bid on each of these auctions (2NT is Ogust)?

1
♠ K Q 10 9 7 5
♥ J 6 2
♦ 9 6
♣ 5 4

Partner	You
	2♠
2NT	?

2
♠ 7 5
♥ A 10 8 6 4 3
♦ K Q 5
♣ 8 5

Partner	You
	2♥
2NT	?

3
♠ A 8 5
♥ A 7 5 3
♦ A 4
♣ A 8 6 3

Partner	You
2♠	2NT
3♦	?

4
♠ 10 7
♥ A Q 9 6
♦ A K Q 6
♣ A Q 8

Partner	You
2♠	2NT
3♥	?

ANSWERS

1   **3♦**   You have a minimum in terms of high cards, but your suit quality is good. 3♦ = a minimum hand, good suit.

2   **3♥**   You have a maximum hand in terms of points, but your suit quality is poor. 3♥ = a maximum hand, poor suit.

3   **3NT**   Partner has shown a minimum with a good suit. He must have at least ♠KQxxxx but he cannot have as much as a king outside his suit. Assuming you can run six tricks in spades, you can count nine tricks. There is a great danger that you will be able to make only the same nine tricks in 4♠. Look at this hand opposite the hand for Problem 1, for example.

4   **4♠**   Partner has a maximum, but as his suit is poor it is unlikely that slam will be a good prospect even with so many HCP.

RESPONSIVE
DOUBLES

Responsive doubles can be used in two similar situations. In both cases LHO has opened with a suit bid and RHO has raised his partner's suit over an intervening bid by your partner. You can decide to play these doubles as responsive to whatever level you choose, but we recommend that playing responsive doubles of raises up to and including 3♠ is sufficient.

These are the two situations in which a double could be played as responsive. In the first scenario, partner has made a takeout double

LHO	*Partner*	*RHO*	*You*
1♠	dbl	2♠	dbl *(responsive)*

while in the second he has made a simple (non-jump) overcall in a suit.

LHO	*Partner*	*RHO*	*You*
1♠	2♥	2♠	dbl *(responsive)*

In both cases, a double of RHO's raise is for takeout, although exactly what it shows will depend on which suits have been bid (as we shall see below).

Why play responsive doubles?

Two bidding problems illustrate the need for responsive doubles. You hold:

LHO	Partner	RHO	You
1♦	dbl	2♦	?

You want to compete since you have four cards in each major and you expect partner to be at least 4-3 in those two suits. The problem, of course, is should you bid 2♥ or 2♠? Partner might easily have either of these hands for his take-out double:

♠ A Q 8 4   ♥ K J 7   ♦ 5   ♣ K J 6 4 3

or

♠ A Q 4   ♥ K J 7 3   ♦ 5   ♣ K J 6 4 3

Obviously, opposite the first hand you want to reach 2♠, while facing the second 2♥ will be a much more comfortable spot. Are you a good guesser? Or would you prefer there were some better way to place the contract? The answer, as you will have gathered, is to make a responsive double. When the opponents have bid and raised a minor suit and partner has made a takeout double, your responsive double simply asks partner to choose his better major.

Similar problems can also arise when partner has overcalled.

LHO	Partner	RHO	You
1♦	1♠	2♦	?

Now a responsive double shows the two unbid suits and a tolerance for partner's suit. You are quite happy to hear partner rebid his spades if he has overcalled on:

♠ A K 9 7 5 2   ♥ Q 5   ♦ 8 5 2   ♣ Q 6

or on

♠ A K J 9 8   ♥ Q 5   ♦ 8 5 2   ♣ A 6 2

However, partner might have something like:

♠ A K 7 4 3   ♥ Q 10 9 3   ♦ 8 5   ♣ Q 6

Now a heart partscore will play very nicely. Or perhaps he has:

♠ A K 7 4 3   ♥ 5   ♦ 8 5 2   ♣ Q J 6 2

Now you want to play in 3♣. By making a responsive double, you tell partner you have support for both hearts and clubs plus a little something in spades, as well as sufficient values to compete. Perfect!

What do you need to make a responsive double?

In all cases, you need sufficient values to compete at the level to which you are driving partner. Opposite a takeout double, this need not be very much. We suggest a minimum of 6 points (including distribution) is sufficient at the 2-level, and 9+ points at the 3-level. These values should be a little higher opposite an overcall, although the better your shape and tolerance for partner's suit, the less high card strength you need. Let's start by looking at the various auctions where partner has made a takeout double.

The requirements for a responsive double after the opponents have bid and raised a minor are straightforward. The auctions are:

LHO	Partner	RHO	You
1♣	dbl	2♣	dbl

and

LHO	Partner	RHO	You
1♦	dbl	2♦	dbl

You need 6+ points (including distribution) and two four-card majors to make a responsive double in each case. This hand would be a typical minimum:

♠ J742   ♥ KQ73   ♦ 82   ♣ 764

Note that you might be much stronger than this, in which case you will raise once partner tells you which major he prefers. If RHO had raised to the three-level instead, you would need at least 9 points and two four-card majors.

LHO	Partner	RHO	You
1♥	dbl	2♥	dbl

This time, as you can usually rely on partner to have four spades for his double of 1♥, you can simply bid 2♠ if you have four of those. The responsive double in this auction is best reserved for hands with support for both minors. On this hand you should simply bid 2♠:

♠ KJ42   ♥ 763   ♦ Q742   ♣ J7

But on this hand, make a responsive double:

♠ Q2   ♥ 763   ♦ QJ92   ♣ KJ73

Partner will choose his better minor: he knows you do not have a four-card spade suit or you would have bid spades. There is a slight difference when the opponents have bid and raised spades:

LHO	Partner	RHO	You
1♠	dbl	2♠	dbl

As above, when the opponents had bid hearts, a double here asks partner to bid his better minor. There is a difference though. When the opponents have hearts, you have a choice of bids when you have spades — 2♠ with a hand that simply wishes to compete for the partscore, and 3♠ when you want to invite partner to bid game. However, when the opponents have bid and raised spades, you obviously only have one heart bid — 3♥ — available below game.

♠ 8 6 4   ♥ K 4   ♦ Q 10 8 3   ♣ A 10 8 5

LHO	Partner	RHO	You
1♠	dbl	2♠	dbl

This would be a classic responsive double in this auction. Partner will choose his better minor. But what about these two hands:

Hand A   ♠ 9 8 6   ♥ Q J 8 6 3   ♦ K 8 3   ♣ K 6

and

Hand B   ♠ 9 8 6   ♥ Q J 8 6 3   ♦ 9 8 3   ♣ K 6

Remember, partner has only promised a minimum opening bid with his double, so you can hardly just up and bid 4♥ on Hand A. However, you would like to invite him to bid game if he has a little extra. On Hand B, you don't want to defend 2♠, but you also don't want to bid 3♥ and hear partner raise to game because he has 14 points rather than 11 or 12.

Hand A   ♠ 9 8 6   ♥ Q J 8 6 3   ♦ K 8 3   ♣ K 6

LHO	Partner	RHO	You
1♠	dbl	2♠	3♥

Again, the way out of this dilemma lies in the use of a responsive double. With the first hand — the one that wants to invite partner to bid game — bid an immediate 3♥. This tells partner that you fully expect to make nine tricks and you would like him to raise if he has something extra for his double.

    With the second hand, the one that just wanted to compete for the partscore, start with a responsive double.

Hand B   ♠ 9 8 6   ♥ Q J 8 6 3   ♦ 9 8 3   ♣ K 6

LHO	Partner	RHO	You
1♠	dbl	2♠	dbl
pass	3♣ or 3♦	pass	3♥

Partner gave preference between the minors, as your double requested, but you now remove yourself to 3♥. This sequence says to partner, 'I want to play in 3♥. Please do not raise unless you are *very* strong'.

When is a double not a responsive double?

There are many auctions that *look* like responsive doubles but are not. To avoid accidents, look at the following auctions and think about why they do not meet the criteria for responsive doubles set out right at the start of this chapter

LHO	Partner	RHO	You
1♦	dbl	2♣	dbl

Your double here is *not* a responsive double as RHO has not raised his partner's suit. He has bid a new suit, one that partner said he has some support for, so double here is for penalties.

LHO	Partner	RHO	You
1♦	1NT	2♦	dbl

This is *not* a responsive double, either. Why not? Because partner has not made a suit overcall. Partner's 1NT shows values in diamonds. Your double is a penalty double, and suggests that RHO has made an error in bidding 2♦.

LHO	Partner	RHO	You
1♦	2♠	3♦	dbl

This is *not* a responsive double because partner has made a weak jump overcall rather than a simple overcall. This is a penalty double.

LHO	Partner	RHO	You
1♦	1♠	4♦	dbl

This is *not* a responsive double because we have agreed to play responsive doubles only as high as 3♠! Even though RHO has raised opener's suit and your partner has made a simple overcall, our responsive doubles stop at 3♠. This one is therefore for penalties.

Summary

✓ A double is responsive when partner doubles a opening bid of a minor and RHO raises opener's suit to the two- or three-level. Your double shows four cards in each major and enough points to compete at the appropriate level (6+ points at the two-level and 9+ points at the three-level)

✓ A double is responsive when partner doubles an opening bid of a major and RHO raises opener's suit to the two- or three-level. Your double shows 9+ points and asks partner to choose between the minors.

✓ After partner doubles an opening 1♠ bid and RHO raises to 2♠, an immediate 3♥ is invitational. If you make a responsive double and then remove partner's minor-suit preference to 3♥ this is strictly competitive — partner is not being asked to bid again.

✓ After partner makes a non-jump overcall in a suit and RHO raises his partner's suit up to and including the level of 3♠, a double is responsive showing support for both unbid suits and a tolerance for partner's suit.

✓ After partner makes any preemptive jump overcall, any double by you is for penalties. Responsive doubles do not apply once partner has preempted.

RESPONSIVE DOUBLES

NOW TRY THESE...

What is your next bid on each of these hands?

1
- ♠ K 9 7 3
- ♥ J 10 4 2
- ♦ 5 4
- ♣ J 7 3

LHO	Partner	RHO	You
1♦	dbl	2♦	?

2
- ♠ K 9 7 3
- ♥ J 10 4 2
- ♦ 5 4
- ♣ J 7 3

LHO	Partner	RHO	You
1♣	dbl	3♣	?

3
- ♠ K 9 7 3
- ♥ J 10 8 4 2
- ♦ 5
- ♣ Q 7 3

LHO	Partner	RHO	You
1♦	dbl	2♦	?

4
- ♠ K J 9 7 3
- ♥ 8 4 2
- ♦ 8
- ♣ 9 8 6 3

LHO	Partner	RHO	You
1♥	dbl	2♥	?

5
- ♠ K Q 8 4 3
- ♥ 8 4 2
- ♦ 8
- ♣ K J 6 3

LHO	Partner	RHO	You
1♥	dbl	2♥	?

6
- ♠ 8 4 3
- ♥ K J 8 6 3
- ♦ 8
- ♣ Q 8 6 3

LHO	Partner	RHO	You
1♠	dbl	2♠	?

7
- ♠ 8 4 3
- ♥ K Q 8 6 3
- ♦ 8
- ♣ K J 6 3

LHO	Partner	RHO	You
1♠	dbl	2♠	?

8
- ♠ J 7 3
- ♥ K 8 6 3
- ♦ 8 3
- ♣ K 10 8 6

LHO	Partner	RHO	You
1♦	1♠	2♦	?

9
- ♠ K 4
- ♥ A Q 7 3
- ♦ 8 6 3
- ♣ K Q 8 3

LHO	Partner	RHO	You
1♦	1♠	2♦	?

10
- ♠ A J 10 8 3
- ♥ K J 9 6
- ♦ A 6 3
- ♣ 4

LHO	Partner	RHO	You
		1♦	1♠
2♦	dbl	pass	?

ANSWERS

1   dbl   You want to compete, so ask partner to choose a major.

2   pass   You are not quite strong enough to force partner to bid at the three-level.

3   2♥   Partner will have at least three card support for both majors so 2♥ will be at least an eight-card fit. Even if he has four cards in each major, 2♥ will be a better contract than 2♠, but if you double, partner might well choose spades. Don't ask him to choose when you have a strong preference.

4   2♠   You don't have very much, but since partner is likely to have four spades and short hearts you do not want to sell out to 2♥.

5   3♠   Good enough to invite game.

6   dbl   This asks partner to choose a minor, but when you remove his choice to 3♥ he will know that you just want to compete and do not want him to raise unless he has significant extra values.

7   3♥   Invitational.

8   2♠   You have three-card support for partner's overcall and a weak hand. Why not tell him exactly that?

9   dbl   You might well want to bid a game, but even if you do, you don't yet know which one. See what partner says after your responsive double.

10   3♥   You have an excellent hand for your overcall and four-card support for the heart suit partner has promised. Because you have three diamonds (and the opponents have at least eight) you know partner has at most two and perhaps a singleton. The hands should fit well and although you may not have the high-card requirements for game, you would expect it to make most of the time.

LEAD-DIRECTING DOUBLES

W H A T ' S   I N   A   N A M E ?

♥ The original concept of using the double of a slam as lead-directing was devised in 1929, by ***Theodore A. Lightner** (1893-1981)* of New York City. Lightner was Life Master #7 and one of America's first World Champions, winning Bermuda Bowl III in 1953. He also partnered Ely Culbertson in international matches against Britain in the 1930's.

You will rarely get rich doubling voluntarily bid slams. Reasonable players only bid slams if they are pretty sure of eleven tricks and have good prospects for the twelfth. It is therefore useful to assign a special meaning to the double of a voluntarily-bid slam: it calls for partner to make an unusual lead — hence the term 'lead-directing double'.

Two examples should suffice to convince you of the mathematical value of playing doubles of slams as lead-directing.

♠ 8   ♥ A 8 6 3   ♦ J 7 2   ♣ A J 7 5 3

LHO	*Partner*	*RHO*	*You*
1♠	pass	3♠	pass
6♠	pass	pass	?

Are you tempted to double? You do have two aces... Before you answer, ask yourself why LHO did not use Blackwood before bidding his slam. The answer you should come up with is that he probably has a void and so the response wouldn't have helped him.

Even if you double and the slam fails by a trick, what have you gained? An extra 50 or 100? If the slam makes because one of your aces doesn't stand up, you will lose an extra 230 (1210 rather than 980 or 1660 rather than 1430) and that doesn't take into account the much larger cost if someone should rudely redouble. It's even worse if you double because you have a trump stack, only to find that you've just given declarer the information he needs to make the hand after all! Now you've traded +100 for -1430, trying to gain an extra 100.

So, doubling just because you think you might be able to beat the hand may not be such a great idea after all. Now look at this hand:

♠ 9 8 4　♥ J 8 7 4 2　♦ —　♣ 9 8 6 4 3

LHO	Partner	RHO	You
1♠	pass	2♦	pass
4♦	pass	4♠	pass
4NT	pass	5♦	pass
6♠	pass	pass	?

If double would ask partner to lead a diamond would you be tempted to double this time? Think about the auction. The opponents have used Blackwood but they have still stopped in a small slam, so they expect to lose one trick (which presumably partner has). They cannot have anticipated losing a diamond ruff too. Even without the assumption that partner has a trick, you will clearly have little chance of beating the slam if you do not get your ruff.

This time, the disadvantage of doubling is the same as above: -230 assuming the opponents do not redouble. However, the potential plus is much better now: +100 rather than -980 or +200 as opposed to -1430. On a really good day, partner will lead a diamond for you to ruff and you will be able to put him back in with his ace to get a second ruff. Now you will score +300 or +500 when on a different lead the opponents would make their slam. Convinced? We thought you would be.

How do Lightner slam doubles work?

A typical lead against a slam would be a suit bid by the defenders, or an unbid suit or a trump. Playing **Lightner doubles**, the double of a voluntarily-bid slam asks for an unusual lead. It specifically tells partner, 'Do not lead any suit we have bid and do not lead a trump'. An 'unusual' lead is usually interpreted as the first suit bid by dummy. If dummy has not bid a suit but declarer has shown a side suit, then the double asks partner to lead that suit. If neither dummy nor declarer has bid a side suit, then the double asks partner to look at the distribution of his hand to judge which suit you are most likely to ruff. (This is not as difficult as it may sound —if you are void in a suit no one has bid, partner will probably have quite a lot of them.)

Of course, in the rare cases when you can be sure of beating the contract on any lead, you can still double. Partner will probably worry about which suit you want him to lead, but it won't matter if you have, for example, the ace and king of trumps.

Can you make a lead-directing double of a game contract?

Yes — the most common situation is when the opponents bid 3NT. A double of a 3NT contract usually calls for a specific lead. If your partner has bid, then the double commands you to lead his suit. For example, he may have KQJ10xx in his suit and an outside ace. He doubles to make sure you lead his suit even if you have a singleton (when you would often otherwise lead your own suit).

If you have bid, then partner's double commands you to lead your own suit. Usually, this occurs when you have bid but the auction has developed in such a way that partner has not had a chance to support you. For example:

LHO	Partner	RHO	You
			1♥
3♠	pass	3NT	pass
pass	dbl	all pass	

Partner will have a good holding in your suit for this double. For example, you might not want to lead away from ♥KJ953 when declarer says he has stoppers. Partner's double suggests he has something like ♥A10x and that declarer has bid 3NT with ♥Qxx or ♥Qxxx in your suit.

If neither you nor partner has bid, then the double of 3NT commands you to lead the first suit bid by dummy, providing that suit was not rebid by dummy or raised by declarer. Finally, if none of the above situations apply, then lead as you would normally lead against a notrump contract. Partner is doubling just because he has a good hand and expects the contract to fail.

What other types of lead-directing doubles are there?

Sometimes a defender will get the chance to make a lead-directing double during the auction, for example, by doubling an artificial bid. Any artificial bid can be doubled to indicate a favorable opening lead. Common examples include Stayman, transfer bids, responses to Blackwood or cuebids.

BY THE WAY

Lead-directing doubles are a fruit-ful area for partnership discussion and agreement. If the opposition use one against you, make sure to ask them what it means.

For example,

LHO	Partner	RHO	You
1NT	pass	2♣	dbl

RHO's 2♣ bid is Stayman. If you have good clubs (say KQJ10x), this is an ideal time to suggest that partner leads a club against the final contract. This is a lead-directing double.

Similarly

LHO	Partner	RHO	You
1NT	pass	2♥	dbl

if 2♥ is a transfer to spades, you can seize the opportunity to double to suggest a heart lead later on.

LHO	Partner	RHO	You
1♥	pass	3♥	pass
4NT	pass	5♦	?

Double the response to Blackwood if you want a diamond lead here. In fact, if partner is agonizing over the lead, he is entitled to take into consideration your failure to double if you had the chance, and will tend to lead something else.

Summary

✓ A double of a freely-bid slam asks partner to make an unusual lead. This is commonly the lead of dummy's first-bid suit. The double specifically forbids the lead of any suit your side has bid or a trump lead.

✓ A double of 3NT asks partner to lead your suit if you have bid one, or to lead his own suit if he has bid one.

✓ Doubles of artificial bids show a desire for partner to lead the bid suit if he is ever on lead.

LEAD-DIRECTING DOUBLES

NOW TRY THESE...

Problems 1-5: do you double, and if so, why? Problems 6-10: what do you lead?

1
- ♠ 9 7 4
- ♥ —
- ♦ J 7 6 5 4 3
- ♣ Q 9 8 4

LHO	Partner	RHO	You
1♠	pass	2♥	pass
3♠	pass	4NT	pass
5♥	pass	6♠	?

3
- ♠ Q J 10 8 6 4
- ♥ —
- ♦ 9 7 4
- ♣ A 9 7 6

LHO	Partner	RHO	You
1♦	pass	1♥	1♠
3♦	pass	4NT	pass
5♦	pass	6♦	?

5
- ♠ Q J 10 9
- ♥ K J 4
- ♦ Q J 7
- ♣ 9 6 3

LHO	Partner	RHO	You
1♠	pass	3♠	pass
6♠	pass	pass	?

7
- ♠ 8 6 4
- ♥ Q J 10 7 5 3
- ♦ 5
- ♣ J 10 7

LHO	Partner	RHO	You
	1♦	2♣	pass
3♣	pass	3NT	pass
pass	dbl	all pass	

9
- ♠ Q 10 7 5
- ♥ J 8 7
- ♦ 10 9 8 5
- ♣ 9 7

LHO	Partner	RHO	You
		1NT	pass
2♣	dbl	2♠	pass
3NT	all pass		

2
- ♠ J 7 5 4
- ♥ A 10 4
- ♦ 8 7 5 3
- ♣ 8 6

LHO	Partner	RHO	You
1♦	1♥	3♦	pass
3NT	pass	pass	?

4
- ♠ K Q J 10 7 4
- ♥ A 4
- ♦ Q J 6
- ♣ 7 3

LHO	Partner	RHO	You
			1♠
1NT	pass	3NT	?

6
- ♠ 9 7 4
- ♥ A 9
- ♦ 9 7 6 5 4 3
- ♣ 5 3

LHO	Partner	RHO	You
	pass	4♠	pass
6♠	dbl	all pass	

8
- ♠ 9 7 4
- ♥ J 8
- ♦ 9 6
- ♣ Q J 9 7 4 3

LHO	Partner	RHO	You
1♥	pass	1♠	pass
3♠	pass	4NT	pass
5♦	dbl	6♠	all pass

10
- ♠ 8 7
- ♥ J 10 9 7 5
- ♦ 9
- ♣ K 10 7 5 3

LHO	Partner	RHO	You
		1♠	pass
1NT	pass	3♣	pass
3♠	pass	4NT	pass
5♦	pass	6♠	pass
pass	dbl	all pass	

ANSWERS

1   **dbl**   This specifically asks partner to lead dummy's first bid suit — hearts. Even a heart lead will not always beat the contract, but you can be fairly sure that no other lead will and it is worth the risk.

2   **dbl**   Partner probably will not lead his broken heart suit unless you tell him to do so. 3NT may still make even on a heart lead, but it will almost certainly do so on any other lead.

3   **dbl**   The opponents are ready for a spade lead, and looking at your hand you can see why. You want a heart lead, to score your ruff, but partner is sure to lead a spade unless you tell him *not* to do so.

4   **dbl**   You must make sure that partner leads a spade. Yes, he might lead one anyway, but if he has a singleton spade and something like ♣Q10xxxx in clubs he is likely to lead a club if you do not double.

5   **dbl**   You do not care what partner leads. 6♠ is going down and you have enough bits and pieces outside not to fear that opponents will run to 6NT and make that.

6   **♦9**   Partner wants a ruff, and looking at your hand you can be fairly sure that it is diamonds in which he is void. Lead the highest diamond as a suit-preference signal so that he will know to return a heart rather than a club to put you back in to get a second ruff.

7   **♦5**   Partner has doubled to make sure you lead his suit. Even the nice heart suit should not dissuade you from doing so. Note that if partner had not doubled, you would have preferred a heart lead rather than a singleton in his minor.

8   **♦9**   Without partner's lead-directing double of 5♦ you would have led a club, but there is no reason to ignore partner's suggestion.

9   **♣9**   Without partner's lead-directing double of 2♣ you would probably have led a diamond. If partner thinks a club lead is best, you certainly have no reason to argue with that.

10   **♣5**   Without partner's double you would have chosen between the safe ♥J and the attacking singleton diamond. Since dummy has not bid a suit, partner's double asks you to lead declarer's second suit — remember, the Lightner Double calls for an *unusual* lead. Partner will surely ruff the club lead, and you will still come to your ♣K later.